SOCIAL TRANSFORMATION OF AN ISLAND NATION : WONDER IN MAURITIUS

SOCIAL TRANSFORMATION OF AN ISLAND NATION

Development Wonder in Mauritius

RANI MEHTA

S.R. MEHTA

KALPAZ

Social Transformation of an Island Nation : Development Wonder in Mauritius

Rs. 690

ISBN: 978-81-7835-811-6

Published in 2010 in India by
Kalpaz Publications
C-30, Satyawati Nagar,
Delhi-110052
E-mail: kalpaz@hotmail.com
Phone : 9212729499

Lasser Type Setting by: Rudra Computer Graphics, Delhi
Printed at : Gian Ridhi Offset Printers, Delhi

Contents

Preface

Development of a group, community or a society is realized either by transforming Men who act as agents of change or by changing the physical and socio-cultural environments in which they are located or placed. Modernization theorists emphasized on the former idea while the political economists stressed on state interventions to improve the environmental conditions so that individuals could change themselves while in interaction with them. Whether one follows a capitalist paradigm or a socialist perspective, both of these have proved inadequate for the development of human groups because of scarcity of resources especially in the context of "new" or developing nations. Further, there is now a stress laid on sustainable development to match the available resources for the development of the future generations.

For the developing nations, there are inherent structural impediments, which are, by and large, the legacies of the colonial regimes. These nations were subjected, for long, to exploitation, oppression and discrimination at the hands of colonial masters who squeezed them of their potential resources and left them high and dry. They had to pursue their own course of action to build them up for advancement and progress, after a long sustained struggle by their political leaders to attain freedom or independence from the colonists.

Mauritius, an island nation, in the Indian ocean is one such country which witnessed slavery and colonial exploitation for more than hundred years before it could attain its independence from the British colonist on March 12, 1968 and acquired a Republic status on the same date in 1992. On our revisit to Mauritius from January to May, 2008 (The first visit was made between July 1975 to March 1980 and the book based on that visit, entitled as "Social Development in Mauritius" was published by Prof. S.R. Mehta), an attempt has been made in this work to understand the dynamics of change and development over a period of nearly three decades on this tiny island nation.

This macro-level study based on documentary evidences or researches carried out by local and foreign social science scholars, has been supplemented by our observations on the different aspects of change and continuity of social-cultural life of people as well as through our interaction with the key informants of the local population in Mauritius at different levels. This could become a possibility because of teaching assignment of Dr. Rani Mehta as a Lecturer in Sociology at the Faculty of Social Studies and Humanities, at the University of Mauritius, Reduit.

We owe a lot to a host of persons who showed enormous generosity in providing to us a lot of published and unpublished material, which formed the basis of this book. We are especially indebted to Ms. Satinder Ragobur, Dean; Dr. Sheilla Bunwaree, Associate Professor, Dr. Raukaya Kasenally, Senior Lecturer and Dr. Shyam Nath, Professor of Economics, all from the Faculty of Social Studies and Humanities at the University of Mauritius for their full support and cooperation in providing us, not only the relevant information but also their published and the other important materials on Mauritius. We are grateful to them for their cordial and warm cooperation.

We are also grateful to Messrs Raj Venkatsamy, K.N. Geerjanand and Prem Toofanny (old colleagues of Dr. S.R. Mehta) for providing us the statistical reports and material on Mauritius besides enriching our thoughts on different issues. They were very warm and helpful during our stay in Mauritius. We would also extend our sincere thanks to Mr. Chit Dukhira, an eminent author of Mauritius, for sharing his views with us and willingly parting with his book on Mauritius as a complimentary copy. We are also thankful to other key informants with whom we interacted at the Mahatma Gandhi Institute, Moka and other places.

We shall be failing in our duty, if we do not extend our heart felt thanks to the worthy Vice Chancellor Prof. R. C. Sobti of Panjab University Chandigarh for his support and encouragement to Dr. Rani Mehta, to carry out this endeavour. We are also thankful to colleagues of Dr Rani Mehta in the Department of Sociology for their kind cooperation. Last, but not least, we are also thankful to Mr. Hari Ram Yadav for his pains taking efforts to type the manuscript and give shape to it in the present form.

Dr. Rani Mehta
Senior Lecturer
Department of Sociology
Panjab University
Chandigarh-160014
India

Professor S.R. Mehta
Former Baba Prithvi Singh Azad Professor in Sociology
Panjab University, Chandigarh and Fellow
Indian Institute of Advanced Study, Rashtrapati Nivas Shimla-5.

1

Introduction

Authors' Note: Mauritius Revisited

The enchanting and bewildering beauty of Ile-de-Maurice (named after Prince Maurice of Holland) has been well described by the famous American author Mark Twain, who after visiting it, wrote in 1897

"You gather the idea that Mauritius was made first and then Heaven, and that Heaven was copied after Mauritius".

If the above quote is to be believed for the existence of the "Concept of Heaven", then one cannot but agree with Mark Twain for the nature bestowing upon this pearl shaped island in the Indian ocean, a heavenly beauty, tranquillity and peace

Mauritius attained independence as a tiny nation from the yoke of British rule, in the year 1968. As a free country, initially it had lot of teething problems as some of the conservative political outfits were against its freedom movement heralded by Labour Party headed by Sir Seewoosagar Ramgoolam, who became its first Prime

Minister. The legacy of underdevelopment left by British colonist was marked by exploitation, discrimination and backwardness of the majority of population characterized by poverty, lack of education, and dismal health and malnourishment etc. However, the leadership at the helm of affairs at the time of independence had vision and the Labour Party in power despite resistance and opposition from certain quarters went ahead with its development policy. To start with, the democratic political structure that adopted the parliamentary system of governance, because of financial crunch, had no alternative but to depend upon the aid-development projects of bilateral and multi-lateral agencies.

One such project funded by the World Bank, was on Rural Development in Mauritius. Perhaps that was the first project of that kind financed by the Bank after Robert McNamera's speech on Poverty in Nairobi, on an experimental basis to evolve its methodologies for the rural development of "new" nations of Asia, Africa and Latin America where most people live in the villages to eke out their existence by having agricultural pursuits of crop production of various types of foods. One of the authors (Shiv. R Mehta) had an opportunity to actively get involved in this project on Rural Development as an expatriate Sociologist and Head of Evaluation from middle of July 1975 to early April, 1980.

This author had a unique chance to spend nearly five years in Mauritius as a Head of an "Evaluation Unit" established within the Rural Development Project. Apart from a book titled **"Social Development in Mauritius: A Study on Rural Modernization in an Island Community" (1981)**, he could generate more than a dozen Operational and Evaluation Studies to assess the result of various components of the development project. A long stint of stay, gave the author a position of advantage in observing the ongoing development processes then in Mauritius. The findings of the data-based study done by the author (published as a book) on a sample basis (832 households were chosen from among a total population of 23,563 households in 28 Villages Council Areas under the project, constituting nearly 3.5 percent sample of the total households) may serve as a baseline for assessing the changes in Economic, Political and Socio-cultural life of people of this Island over a period of nearly three decades.

The present visit to Mauritius (from January to May 2008) could materialize as a dream come true due to Rani Mehta (author) getting an appointment as a Lecturer to teach Sociology at Faculty of Social Studies and Humanities at the University of Mauritius. (Incidentally, the two years assignment could not be completed and she had to return to her present Department of Sociology at Panjab University, Chandigarh after teaching in Mauritius for one semester due to compelling reasons of theft and burning of part of the house by thieves back-home.) Rani was born in Mauritius while her father, Shiv R. Mehta, was on assignment in Mauritius during 1975-80. However, when Rani went to Mauritius in the year 2008, she was accompanied by her parents and this present study is an effort of the daughter-father duo in collecting relevant information and studies pertaining to the processes of change and development in Mauritius over a period of three decades or so. The credit for generation of wealth of material for this study goes to Rani Mehta. Not only, she could collect relevant published, unpublished, books/ articles or papers from her colleagues in the Faculty of Social Studies and Humanities but the feedback she could get from her students, further enriched the material for this study.

Rani was a small kid and Shiv R. Mehta (her father) was in the middle age when both returned to India in 1980 from Mauritius. Our revisit to Mauritius in 2008 for five months or so, was a chance that we would not like to miss. We were keen to visit Mauritius and study the changing character of an emerging society. The unfolding of pages in this script and response of readers to them shall show whether or not, we have succeeded in our objective in carrying out a sociological study of a changing society.

Conceptual Framework of the Study

"Unlike the natural scientists, who may be thought of applying concepts to things, the sociologists seek to apply concepts to the understanding of social relations, and social relations in turn depend upon the conceptualisations which actors make of their world and of other actors" (John Rex, 1970). Empirical verification of a social phenomenon or a series of phenomena has become the hallmark of sociological investigations. It is also recognized quite lately that building up of social constructs or formulation of concepts related to understanding or analysis of social events, issues or problems is becoming slight. This has sensitised some sociologists to vouch for a serious attempt on their part to conceptualise a social phenomenon before its examination. Despite policy implications of sociological configurations for mitigating a social problem, pure empiricism may tend to become "Pop Sociology" in the perception of Giddens (1996). He advocates that sociology as a knowledge building exercise, must have serious inputs of conceptual framework for understanding or explaining the social phenomenon and the sociologist should strive hard towards that end to prevent the decaying of the discipline.

In the above backdrop, as sociologists we are seized with the problem of looking for a conceptual framework that should provide understanding of and explanations for a changing community or society. Since sociology as a discipline has a Euro-American tradition, the conceptual formulations have been immensely influenced by enlightenment thinkers, philosophical foundations, epistemological methods and hermeneutics. In physical or biological sciences, we have exact laws postulated to explain various natural phenomena but in analysing a societal system (because of varied complexities and uncertainties) it may be extremely difficult to identify the exact patterns of interaction, between social actors whose relationships are contingent upon "significant others", personality correlates, situations and intensity of interaction. Further, these are influenced by patterns of agencies and institutions in which the interactions take place over time and space and on the external environment in which the internal system is located (Mehta, 1999).

Notwithstanding the limitation of sociological perspectives to explain the phenomena of social change and development (Both the "Modernization" paradigm and Neo-Marxist political economy model (Dependency Theory and World System Theory) have failed to tackle the problems of poverty, unemployment and income disparities in the developing societies Coleman (1991) advocates a Constructed Theory of Social Change for a changing society. In his prologue to an edited volume with Bourdieu, based on a conference "Social Theory and Emerging Issues in a Changing Society", he makes a reference to this change from primordial and spontaneous social organizations (family, clan, ethnic, group, religious groups based on traditional relationships) to a constructed social organization, constructed for either a single purpose or a narrow range of purposes (proto-type is the formal organization composed of positions established by the person or persons who constructed the organization). In such an organization, the rules, the expectations and obligations between positions and incentive structure for individuals are not evolved spontaneously as is done in a primordial organisation but these are determined by the persons who design such a type for a social organisation. The social control in the primordial organization is provided by values and sanctions thrown up by social and cultural imperatives embedded in it including formal laws based on such principles. However, in the individualistic society or constructed social organization, it is provided by law and its formal means of enforcement. But, this formal law enforcement is not a sufficient solution for a well functioning normative system, influenced both by internalised sanctions and informed external sanctions. A work-group collective supervision to accomplish the goal of such an organization by having suitable structural conditions to induce incentives may help in establishing an organization similar to a spontaneous one. In the constructed social organization, another problem confronted is distribution of social product as most of the economic exchange of goods and services has moved out in a double exchange economy, labour for money and money for exchange of goods and services.

A suitable mechanism needs to be evolved by the constructed organization to institutionalise the large number of dependent individuals outside the purview of distributions of abundance in a developed or developing economy for greater equality among its people. Can it be achieved by redistributions after first round of distribution by the market, that is, allocation of wages and income? One way may be to revive communal redistribution to implement primary distributions through the double exchange economy, which is a difficult proposition. The alternative way could be to create around the individual new focus of social capital, that is, micro-social institutions through the social psychological incentive found effective in the institution of family.

The control system of a constructed social organization shall have to choose out of the above alternatives for its growth or development. This holds good and has significant relevance for a developing society. It is well recognized now that economic theory has a stronger explanatory power to analyse the production and consumption behaviour of people but it is weak in regard to its explanation, so far its distribution of goods is concerned. Perhaps, this theory needs re-examination to provide equity, social justice and probity to those in the society who are marginalized for being excluded from the market distribution system.

In the above backdrop, it becomes increasingly problematic when one is interested in analysing a pluralistic society having mixed population of different ethnic stocks, mostly drawn in as a consequence of migration from various parts of the world by the dominant minority to pursue economic activities for growth and development. For development of a pluralistic society, all the constituents of its population within a territorial area must get an equal share of distribution of goods and services generated within or outside it. But, in reality it does not take place in a dual exchange economy (labour for money and money for exchange of goods and services) as the conception of self-sufficiency of a society has become absurd in an increasingly conceived view of a society as an overlapping process system in the contemporary sense. It is argued that such a society will not be self-contained, as it will overlap with the other society.

In the above context, there is a need to understand the concept of plural societies which, more often than not, are having primordial based social organizations mediated and permeated by customs, mores, conventions and laws evolved therein, to promote cooperation between competing groups to make them a viable proposition and a functioning reality. Before we dwell on such societies in detail, it would be apt to make a distinction between the society and other groupings in it. For example, one such grouping identified is community, which has been used in a variety of ways. Some scholars view communities as local units of a larger society while others consider them as pertaining to the solidarity dimension such as communal or spatial.

As such, it would be inadequate to confine the sociological analysis of society to the realm of national boundary and keep it closed completely from the imposition of the emergent global level influences. In fact, in the last few decades, we have entered in an era of information society, giving rise to the concept of society as a global "village" where the holders of media of communication are the key players in manipulating and controlling money and power, thus making the concept of national sovereignty in conceptualising a society, circumscribed by a territory, absurd (Mehta, 2005). Even, then, the concept of community cannot be whisked away that easily. It is a meso-level that connects micro level (individual) to macro level (society) in establishing social relationship between the three levels to constitute a composite social structure and culture of a given population. In fact, in the transitional phase of development of the developing societies, there is a paradox of traditional coexisting with the modern in the social life of people as on one side, we want to maintain our cultural traditions while on the other, we would like to catch up with the lifestyle of the developed societies.

Many sociological analysis, pertain to the movement of community to society as the human relationships become more complex, intricate and knotty and are based on formal social arrangements of agents, agencies and institutions. We cannot ignore the contribution in this regard by a German Sociologist, Ferdinand Tonnies (1895) who coined the concepts of Gemeinschaft and Gesellschaft, the former construct pertaining to the characteristics of community while the latter focussing on that of society. We shall discuss these concepts as they have relevance to the developing societies, moving from traditional to modern social structures (This dichotomous classification of society has also been conceptualised by other sociologists in term of mechanical-organic solidarities, ideal-types, traditional-modern, inner directed-outer directed, bourgeois-proletariat (Class-Classless societies).

According to Tonnies (1955, 1895) human relations are based in mutual actions. As such, he focuses on relationships of mutual affirmation, resulting into an association both as real and organic or as imaginary and mechanical in character. The former is the essential characteristic of the Gemeinschaft (Community) while the latter is denoting Gesellschaft (Society). Whereas all intimate, private and exclusive living is considered as life in Gemeinschaft while Gesellschaft (society) has a predominance of public life. It is observed that Gemeinschaft in rural life among people is stronger and more alive mainly because of lasting and genuine form of living together and has to be understood as an example of living organism whereas Gesellschaft is transitory, superficial, a sort of mechanical aggregated artefact. The Gemeinschaft based on blood or unity of being, is differentiated from that based on locality or common habitat or from that of mind; implying only cooperative and coordinated action for a common goal. It is pointed out that "Wherever human beings are related through their wills in an organic manner and affirm each other, we find one or another of the three types of Gemeinschaft; the definite and meaningful derivations of the original categories of Gemeinschaft are kinship, neighbourhood and friendship".

In the context of village and town, the common principle of social organization is determined by space rather than time, which predominates through the generations of the family, the tribe and the people. The family appears to have some invisible metaphysical roots because it is believed to descend from common ancestors, as if they were hidden in the earth. Besides, the living individuals in the family are connected with each other by the sequence of past and future generations. However, the strongest ties and relations in a village and town, are created by the physical real soil, the permanent location and the visible land. In fact, during the period of Gemeinschaft, (Community) "the younger principle of space remains bound to the older principle of time".

However, in the Gesellschaft period, this gets disconnected and results into the development and growth of a city. The principle of space gets more pronounced and exaggerated in urban as contrast to the rural form, which is essentially bound to both the principles of space and time. It is in this sense, the whole continual development is considered as a process of increasing urbanization. Tonnies sums up the shift from Gemeinschaft to Gesellschaft by making a reference to Karl Marx's Das Kapital I, which points out, "It may be said that the whole economic history of Gesellschaft, that is, of the modern nations, is in essence summarized in the change in the relationship between town and country." In other words, towns/cities acquire predominance over the rural organizations which need to use their productive forces to support the furtherance and strengthening of the urban areas. (Tonnies, 1955, 1895).

The above conceptions of Gemeinschaft (Community) and Gesellschaft (Society) are significant in analysing a changing society. Having understood the characteristics of these constructs by Tonnies, it may be apt to examine the conceptions of plural economies and societies, as with the growth and development of nation-states, due to migrations and "pull" and "push" factors of migrations, these nations, over the years acquire a pluralistic population character. People are drawn into a national territory from the different regions of the world having distinct cultural, linguistic and religious diversities either to eke out their existence or to make fortune. (Western thinkers consider society as prior to and outside the state but Hobbes treats the social contract, the law of nature and the civil society as identical. However, Locke makes a distinction between the law of nature and the social contract that formed the state. He thinks that there is a natural order assured by man's interdependence and his natural rights for all. It existed prior to and outside the political institution. The state is an utilitarian device for providing a more efficient, less cumbersome social order by having a specialized apparatus to enforce the natural law.)

Plural societies are conceived to be more heterogeneous than homogeneous in population composition, social arrangements, cultural norms and values, consumption patterns, stratification patterns and are guided mainly by their respective traditions and social organizations in establishing human relations with different people. This gives rise to various kinds of contradictions and conflicts in social relationships and mutual understandings or orientations. In fact, the social and cultural capacities of individuals or groups to build up relationships across different segments of population in a territorial region, being variant, brings in an element of distrust, bias and prejudice against each other and that results in an uneven appropriation of economic resources by different groups. As a consequence of that, there is marginalization of certain groups who face impoverishment at the hands of elite groups (even minority dominant groups) and individuals.

As has been mentioned by Smith (1965), Furnivall, J.S. (1939) was the first to distinguish the plural society as a separate form of society. Before we take up Smith's views on social and cultural pluralism, it may be appropriate to delineate the concept of plural economies wherein Furnivall has discussed plural societies, the plural state and social demand characteristics. Netherlands India (now Indonesia) is mentioned as a typical of tropical dependencies as an example of a plural society, comprising two or more elements or social orders, living side by side without mingling under one political unit (the rulers and the ruled belonging to different races). But we have a plural society also in independent states such as Siam where Natives, Chinese and Europeans —have distinct economic functions and live apart as separate social orders. Even in South Africa and the United States of America, there are both white and coloured populations. So is the case of a plural society in the French provinces of Canada where two peoples are separated by race, language and religion (Furnivall, 1939).

Examining the significant characteristics of the economic aspects of social organization in a plural society, Furnivall points out that in it, there is no common will except in matters of supreme importance such as resistance to aggression from the outside. In political sense, a plural society is a confederation of allied provinces, united by treaty or within the limits of a formal constitution for having certain ends common to the constituent units but outside the term of Union, each living in its own life. However, it is different from the confederation, in the sense that the constituent elements are not segregated within its territorial limits. In a confederation, secession is at least possible without complete disruption of all social bonds but in a plural society, the elements are so intermingled that secession is identical with anarchy. Further, in economic life, this lack of a common will, which characterizes plural societies, has no common social demand. Political economists while dealing with political economy emphasize on production, exchange and distribution of wealth but express a little about consumption except by way of speaking about aggregate and joint demand. However, these are different from social or collective demand as the will of all differs from the general will.

It is observed that every political society evolves its own civilization and distinctive culture, ethos, religious creeds, art forms (literature, painting, sculpture and music), conventions in daily life more so through informal than formal instructions or education and each citizen is moulded as a member of that society. In this process, we develop social wants, which he or she experiences as a member of that society and can satisfy them only as a member of that. As such, the religious, political and aesthetic and the cultural aspects of life do not come within the scope of economics. However, all cultural needs have an economic aspect because they find organized manifestation only in economic wants and demands. In other words, every social want has its economic aspect reflected through economic dimension of its civilization or the social demand of a community as a whole.

But, it is argued that in a plural society, social demand is disorganized because social wants are sectional as no social demand common to all tie various elements. In fact, this disorganization of social demand raises the economic criterion, a new place in a scale of social values, as the different sectors of a plural society are bound to meet the common market place. In that sense, the highest common factor of their wants is the economic factor despite their cultural or ethnic differences. This shifts the emphasis on production rather than on social demand and leads to sectional division of labour, promoting economic castes, having conflict of interest within each community, to be resolved by having a common citizenship to constitute a homogeneous society But, in a plural society, each community or group lives within a closed compartment and life within each section tends to become narrower. Further, the community gets organized for production rather than for social life. As social demand gets sectionalised within each section of the community, it becomes disorganized and ineffective and members of each section get debarred from having a full life of a citizen in a homogeneous community (Furnivall, 1939)

In the above backdrop, a plural society remains, by and large, heterogeneous in form and structure. One may observe that even Furnivall in his conception of a plural society is aware of the fact that it has within it, several closed groups or communities and relationships within or even between them are primarily determined by primordial ties based on traditional cultural practices and social arrangements. Smith (1965) strengthens this aspect by highlighting that as observed by Furnivall, economic pluralism was simply an aspect of the social pluralism of various colonies and he, even, correlates this with cultural pluralism. He opines that the core of culture is its institutional system and each institution is formulated by set forms of activity, grouping, rules, ideas and values. The total system of institutions is having three interdependent systems of action, idea and value and social relations. It is further, observed that institutions dealing within the same phase of life form a systematic cluster. For example marriage, family, levirate, extended kinship forms and the like constitute the kinship subsystem. Also government is the sub-system of regulative institutions such as law, parliament, police and civil and military administration. These sub-systems have many links with each other and it is observed that consistency, interdependence and coherence are greater, within each institutional sub-system than between them. These sub-systems contribute towards the formation of an institutional system. Societies tend to differ in the distribution and complementarity of institutional forms but any institutional system may provide an internal integration and to some extent a closure. As such, in a culturally divided society, each cultural group has its own relatively exclusive way of life based on distinctive system of action, ideas and values and social relations besides being different in language, material culture and technology. Smith is of the view that the culture concept has a much wider connotation than society since it includes conventions, language and technology. However, "the presence of two or more culturally distinct groups within a single society shows that these two aspects of social reality may vary independently in their limits and interrelations."

We do observe that modern societies are culturally heterogeneous in terms of occupational specialities depicting stratification and class differences, ethnic minorities or rural-urban differential way of life. Though modern societies are termed pluralistic because of occupational diversities, yet Smith prefers the term pluralism for these societies, which are culturally heterogeneous, exhibiting formal diversity in the basic system of compulsory institutions such as kinship, education, religion, property and economy, recreation and sodalities. Thus, cultural pluralism, in essence, represents differentiation based in institutional divergencies.

No doubt, the institutional incompatibility gets pronounced by differences of grouping, norms, activities and functions but the monopoly of power by one cultural group is the necessary precondition for the maintenance of the total society. In fact, the structural position and function of the regulative system differ sharply in plural and other societies in the sense that the dominant social group in such culturally heterogeneous societies controls the apparatus of power and force while the sub-ordinate groups regulate their internal affairs independently of their superiors, so long they do not present any threat to the current social order and their customs are tolerated by the dominant majority. It is mentioned that the differing sectional values within a plural society present a source of instability in any political form and these necessitate political changes, usually violent in form, to effect changes in the social structure (Smith, 1965).

The conceptual frameworks analysed in the foregoing pages, point out that Tonnies's concepts of Gemeinschaft and Gesellschaft depicting the constructs of "Community" and "Society" for a changing society are relevant for a study of such a nature of an Island nation that got its physical entity by populations migrating voluntarily or involuntary from across the globe. Again, these concepts need to be put within the perspective of constructed theory of social change, where social organization based on primordial social ties and cultural forms move to a modern corporate organization guided by rules and regulations based on an individual's performance, achievement, merit, social justice, equitable distribution of goods and services, within a democratic rather than autocratic governance and control system.

Further, the conception of cultural pluralism as an all encompassing one, (Smith) beyond the concept of plural society (Furnivall) emphasising on economic pluralism, is relevant for such a study of a population delimited in a territorial area drawn in from different ethnic stocks of Europe, Asia and Africa, speaking different languages, belonging to different racial compositions, following different religious adherences, drawn in through forced or voluntary migrations to pursue economic activities for their survival, sustenance and growth. While adhering to their respective cultural customs and practices, they maintained their cultural identities. Over the years, they established their social relationships between different groups or communities and heralded a political struggle against the dominant political system to attain independence. Besides, they opted for a democratic governance encouraging wider participation of different ethnic groups to move towards a societal formation with new outlook, modern institutional arrangements and values. Of course, in this process of social and economic transformation, the cultural ends, ideas and values need to be analysed as the shifting of values is partial and a paradox of traditional co-existing with the modern way of life, still keeps the option of a full blown society, a far fetched social reality.

In short, the Tonnies's conception of Gemeinschaft and Gesellschaft and Smith's concept of cultural pluralism as an added dimension of plural society by Furnivall, shall be employed in the analysis of this study as and where these shall have relevance for an understanding and explaining of a phenomenon or series of phenomena.

Methods of the Study

The methodology involved in carrying a study should correspond well with the conceptual framework chosen for the same as theory and method should go together. A study of changing society like Mauritius (An Island Country) which has the Gemeinschaft (Community) and Gesellschaft (Society) as two ideal conceptual frameworks presenting the polar opposite characteristics should be diachronic in nature, to be carried out at two points of time. Perhaps it would have been feasible for an "insider" researcher as an indigenous sociologist and anthropologist to analyse the continuities and changes in the Mauritian social structure as he or she being a part of the Island location for long, could do so conveniently at two different points of time. However, for an "outsider" researcher, that possibility becomes a rare opportunity and he or she has to depend upon a synchronic study, to be carried out at one point of time. The debate about "insiders" vis-à-vis "outsiders" for research of sociological nature has been well brought out by Merton, R.K. 1972. Both the methodological approaches have their own advantages and disadvantages. But for the total understanding of the continuities and changes of social structure of a group, community or society, it would be better if these are analysed by the researchers of the "insiders" and "outsiders" types, for an adequate understanding and explanation of various social and cultural phenomena.

In the above context, the present study may be viewed as synchronic in nature as the analysis and findings presented in it are based on the material gathered by the authors during January to May 2008. This could become a possibility when Rani Mehta, one of the authors, got an opportunity to teach sociology at the University of Mauritius. Her interaction with her colleagues and students in different courses she taught (Sociology of Development, Social Stratification and Race and Ethnicity) provided her insights into various changes observed in the Mauritian society. Apart from her interaction with the students and colleagues, the feedback she got from the students through the term paper assignments on different topics of sociological significance relevant to their societal setting enriched her understanding of this society which appears equally influenced by both the external and internal socio-political economic and cultural environments. Besides her general observations on the ongoing processes of development of the Mauritian Society, she also got an opportunity to evaluate research dissertations done by students on different sociological topics relevant to various socio-cultural, political and economic life of people. Moreover, it was possible through her good contact and rapport with her colleagues in the faculty, to collect the published as well as the unpublished materials written by them (Books, Research Reports, Papers, Articles) as well as the other available material written by scholars other than the engaged faculty at the University of Mauritius. In this way, we were able to collect a wealth of information on the social, cultural, political and economic life of the people as a part of the one shot (synchronic) study. It was in 1975, that the other author, Shiv R. Mehta visited Mauritius and continued there till 1980 (July 1975 to March 1980). In that sense, the present study to a certain extent may be considered as diachronic in nature. Not only he could generate a number of operational and evaluation studies on the project (15 of them) but also wrote a book (Social Development in Mauritius, 1981). This data based study inter-alia focused on the stratification pattern and power structure prevailing in the rural areas, institutional analysis of family, marriage and status of women, religion and village organizations and aspects of development and change, highlighting people's values, reactions to development activities, attitudes, education, aspiration for children, political knowledge and other related variables.

The present work is reproduced practically by including some factors such as economic development, political dynamics and socio-cultural aspects of life of people especially those related to social institutional arrangements such as family, marriage, status of women, religion and ethnic relationships. Though, the present book provides a more macro-level scenario than local village based analysis on a sample basis, yet in the context of Mauritius, the rural-urban divide is minimal. In fact, the rural areas have now been considerably modernized in terms of better housing and other infrastructural facilities such as roads, electricity, health care and schools etc.

Interestingly, the data based study by Shiv R. Mehta (1981) calls it an "Island Community" while in contrast many earlier studies have titled their work on Mauritius as a "pluralistic society" (Benedict, 1961, Mannick, 1979). The earlier studies were perhaps, influenced by the conception of "plural society" advocated by Furnivall (1939). However, during his stay, Shiv R. Mehta felt that the immediate post-independent period in Mauritius had not yet acquired a societal structure as most of the social relationships among people were based more on primordial ties such as ethnic, religious, social and cultural codes, residential patterns and kinship networks than on formal codes, rules and regulations and modern institutional arrangements, though these aspects were emerging and maturing. In view of the above, the book title emphasized it as an "island community" than a "plural society". This type of observation got confirmed when one of the authors (Shiv R. Mehta) in his second visit (January to May, 2008) while interacting with a Professor of Economics at the University of Mauritius, was told that "When you visited Mauritius first (1975-80), it was a sort of village but now it was evolving as a society". On reflection of this remark, it was thought best to place the present work within the Gemeinschaft (Community) and Gesellschaft (Society) continuum. Instead of treating the social aspects of life in polar opposite positions, some of the institutional systems as core of the cultural life may be operating side by side in this changing community or society.

No doubt, cultural pluralism is still a social reality of this emerging plural society, yet one is not sure, whether or not the process of the ethnic cultural differences between various groups is getting less pronounced and giving way to strict socio-economic and class structure. Some of the issues related to the above processes of change shall be examined in this work.

In short, one may venture to say that this study is, basically, a documentary research based on books, research reports, Census data, published and unpublished articles, papers and reports of scholars (insiders as well as outsiders).

Further, these have been supplemented adequately by interaction with a larger number of key informants in different strata of the Mauritian society and by observations made on different aspects of development including infrastructural, institutional, technological, participative and social service oriented changes in this small nation over the years. It is hoped that the findings of this study shall provide significant leads to the development planners of the country to formulate social policies for its progress and prosperity.

References

Benedict, Burton (1961), *Indians in a Plural Society*, London, HMSO (Her Majesty Service Overseas).

Bourdieu, Pierre and Coleman, James S (1991) (Eds). *Social Theory for a Changing Society*, New York, Western Press, Russell Sage Foundation.

Furnivall, J.S. (1939) *Netherlands India: A Study of Plural Economy*: Cambridge University Press.

Giddens Anthony (1996) *In Defence of Sociology: Essays, Interpretations and Rejoinder*, Cambridge, Polity Press.

Mannick, A.R. (1979), *Mauritius, The Development of a Plural Society* Nottingham, Spokeman.

Merton, R.K. (1972), "Insiders and Outsiders: A Chapter in Sociology of Knowledge". *American Journal of Sociology*, Vol. 78 pp. 9-47.

Mehta, S.R. (1981), *Social Development in Mauritius: A Study on Rural Modernization in an Island Community*, New Delhi, Wiley Eastern Ltd.

Mehta, S. R. (1999), *Dynamics of Development: A Sociological Perspective*, New Delhi, Gyan Publishing House.

Mehta, S. R. (2005), "The Conceptual Journey of Society" *Summer Hill IIAS Review* Vol. XI, No. 1, Shimla, Indian Institute of Advanced Study.

Rex, John. (1970) *Race Relations in Sociological Theory*, Routledge and Kegan Paul.

Smith, M.G.(1965) *The Plural Society in the British West Indies*, University of California Press.

Tonnies, Ferdinand (1895, 1955) *Community and Society*, Routledge, Kegan Paul.

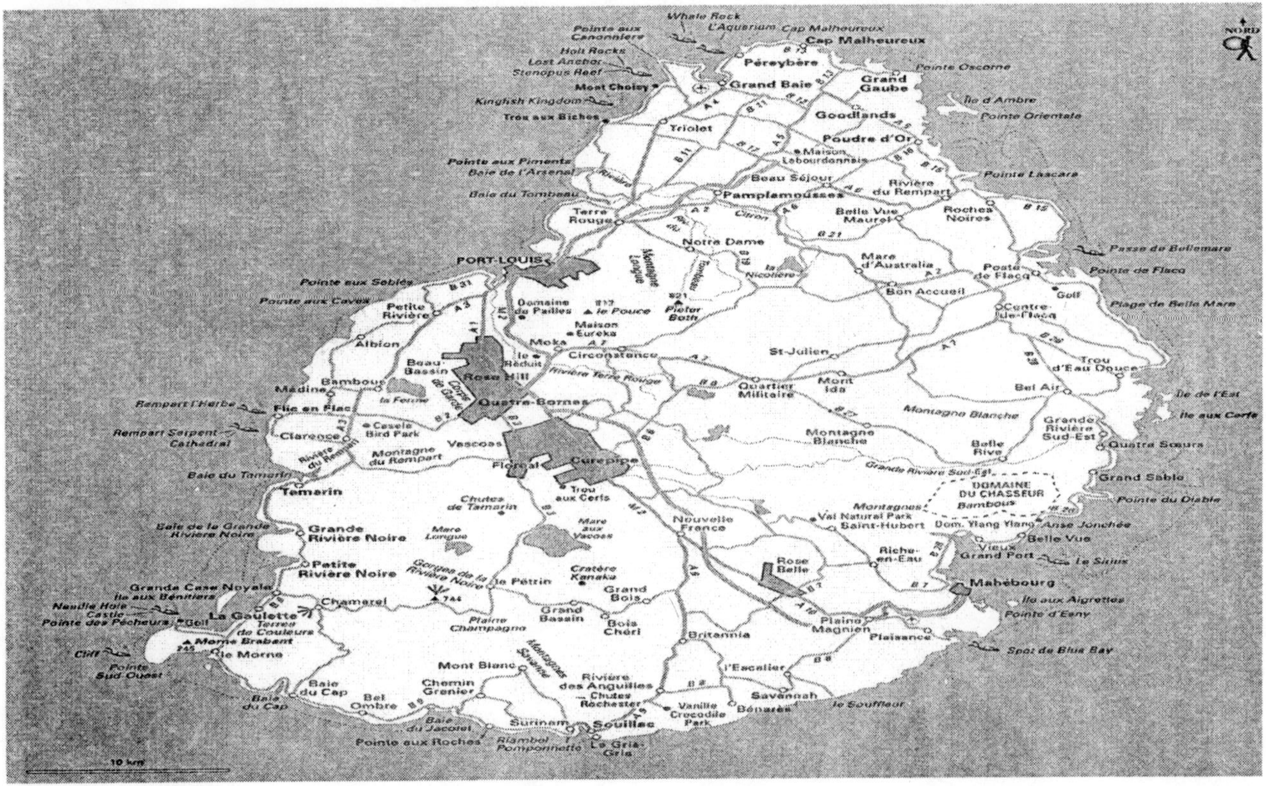
NORD
Whale Rock
L'Aquarium
Cap Malheureux
Pointe aux Canonniers
Holt Rocks
Lost Anchor
Stenopus Reef
Mont Choisy
Kingfish Kingdom
Trou aux Biches
Péreybère
Grand Baie
Grand Gaube
Pointe Oscorne
Île d'Ambre
Pointe Orientale
Goodlands
Triolet
Poudre d'Or
Maison Lebourdonnais
Pointe aux Piments
Baie de l'Arsenal
Baie du Tombeau
Beau Séjour
Rivière du Rempart
Pointe Lascars
Pamplemousses
Terre Rouge
Citron
Belle Vue Maurel
Roches Noires
Notre Dame
Montagne Longue
Tombeau
PORT-LOUIS
Mare d'Australia
Poste de Flacq
Passe de Bellemare
Pointe de Flacq
la Nicolière
Bon Accueil
Golf
Pointe aux Sables
Pointe aux Caves
Petite Rivière
Domaine de Pailles
le Pouce
Pieter Both
Centre de Flacq
Plage de Belle Mare
Maison Eureka
Albion
Moka
le Réduit
Circonstance
St-Julien
Trou d'Eau Douce
Beau Bassin
Rose Hill
Corps de Garde
Bambous
Médine
Rivière Terre Rouge
Quartier Militaire
Mont Ida
Bel Air
la Ferme
Quatre-Bornes
Île de l'Est
Rempart l'Herbe
Flic en Flac
Montagne Blanche
Île aux Cerfs
Casela Bird Park
Rempart Serpent
Cathedral
Clarence
Vacoas
Montagne Blanche
Grande Rivière Sud-Est
Montagne du Rempart
Rivière du Rempart
Belle Rive
Quatre Sœurs
Floréal
Curepipe
Baie du Tamarin
Grande Rivière Sud-Est
Grand Sable
Tamarin
DOMAINE DU CHASSEUR
Trou aux Cerfs
Chutes de Tamarin
Montagnes Bambous
Pointe du Diable
Baie de la Grande Rivière Noire
Grande Rivière Noire
Mare Longue
Mare aux Vacoas
Nouvelle France
Val Natural Park
Saint-Hubert
Dom. Ylang Ylang
Anse Jonchée
Belle Vue
Petite Rivière Noire
Gorges de la Rivière Noire
le Pétrin
Cratère Kanaka
Rose Belle
Riche-en-Eau
Vieux Grand Port
Le Sirius
Grande Case Noyale
Île aux Bénitiers
Grand Bois
Mahébourg
Île aux Aigrettes
Needle Hole
Castle
Pointe des Pêcheurs
Golf
La Gaulette
Chamarel
744
Terres de Couleurs
Plaine Champagne
Grand Bassin
Bois Chéri
Britannia
Plaine Magnien
Pointe d'Esny
Plaisance
Morne Brabant
245
Le Morne
Cliff
Pointe Sud Ouest
Spot de Blue Bay
Mont Blanc
Montagnes Savanne
l'Escalier
Baie du Cap
Chemin Grenier
Rivière des Anguilles
Chutes Rochester
Savannah
Bel Ombre
Vanille Crocodile Park
Bénarès
le Souffleur
Baie du Cap
Baie du Jacotet
Surinam
Souillac
Pointe aux Roches
Riambel
Pomponnette
Le Gris-Gris
10 km

2

Profile of Mauritius

Geographical Location

Mauritius is believed to have been created by a volcano, which is now an extinct crater. This diminutive island is reported to be 40 miles long and 30 miles wide covering an expanse of 120 square miles. Located in the broad Indian Ocean, it is 500 miles away from Madagascar, 1250 miles from the east coast of Africa and 6000 miles from Europe.

This island is bespangled with evergreen trees among its green sugarcane fields. Besides, there are emerald lagoons protected by coral reef that mirror the vast blue sky. Its mountains present some unfamiliar outline towards the sky, depicting different shades varying from blue to mauve and from pink to copper under the caressing sun. Although, it is a volcanic outcome, yet the island has complete harmony with its serene landscapes, blonde beaches and natural beauty. On the world map, it is a dot located in the South West of Indian Ocean between latitudes 19°58′-20°31′ South and 57°17′-57°48′ East. It enjoys a sub-tropical climate with the summer season running from November to April and winter from May to October. It has an average summer temperature of 27°C in the coast and 22°C in the Central region and a winter temperature averaging 18.5°C on the coast and 16°C elsewhere. Its location in the South-West of Indian Ocean, which is a cyclonic zone, makes it prone to sturdy trade winds of moderate intensity blowing from South, East to East-South-East. Further, the land rises from the coastal plain to a central plateau varying in altitude from 900 feet to 2400 feet. There are three mountain ranges which border the plateau and their peaks are in the North, West and South. The highest point on the island at 2711 feet is in the West.

The main dependency of Mauritius is Rodrigues, which is located at 300 miles East as a lovely outpost.

History

A historical account of a place or event is significant as it is the past that influences the present whereas it is the present that shapes the future. In this context, the historical account of Maurituis, which ranges from 1488 AD to 1968, will exhibit the different vicissitudes through which Mauritius has passed before it could attain Independence as a nation.

A Portuguese sailor by the name of Bartholomew Dias writing the history of commercial sea route between Europe and Asia known as the "Spice Route", unknowingly also wrote about Mauritius, which was then uninhabited. Later on, it became an important commercial route between Europe and Asia. An old map of 1502 A.D. showed the presence of Mascarene islands in this part of the region which had Arabian names, for example Mauritius was known as Dina Arabi, Rodrigues as Dina Morase and Reunion as Dina Margabim. Only in the beginning of 16th Century, we have a recorded evidence of human presence. After the arrival of first wave of Portuguese, they gave the island its former name Ihla do Cerne (Swan Island). It was only towards the end of 16th century that the Dutch ventured in the commercial conquest of the East. They were guided and encouraged by Maurice Van Nassan and could build up a strong merchant navy. Later on, it developed into a very powerful mercantile force in the world during the 17th century. Again in 1598, Vice Admiral Wybrant Van Warwijck along with his men landed in what is known now as the Grand Port Bay.

The Dutch got an opportunity to explore the island and called it Mauritius after the name of their prince, Maurice Van Nassan. The first attempt to colonize this place began in 1638 when the first batch of settlers came over there. They stayed for 20 years after which the Dutch decided to vacate the island in 1658 and settled in their new colony in the Cape of "Good Hope". However, in 1664, they tried to colonize it again and met with more degree of success than before as they could do agricultural development on the Mauritian soil by growing sugarcane, rice, indigo and tobacco, besides breeding cattle. But, a very strong cyclone in 1695 destroyed their infrastructure. As a result of that, the Dutch Government took the decision to leave the island and the last group of settlers left in 1710.

It was in the beginning of the 17th century that the King of France delegated full powers to the French East India Company to capture territories and establish colonies in the name of French kingdom. Incidentally, when the Dutch were leaving Mauritius, the French people were already present in the Bourbon island, that is, the present Reunion island and also in Madagascar. It was on September 20, 1715, a captain by the name Guillarime Durfresne d'Arcel arrived at Port Nord-Quest (presently known as Les Salines in Port Louis) and after hoisting the French flag on the Mauritian soil, gave it the name of Isle-de-France. However, the first settlers came only in 1721 and the island witnessed a rapid development after the arrival of Governor Mahe de La Bourdonnais in 1735.

During his 12 years of administration, the island witnessed a rapid development especially in Port Louis. The Governor left the island in 1747 but by that time he had established it as an important naval base and the capital of French East India Company in the Indian Ocean. As a result of construction on the island and other development activities, it also became a center of slave trade. Thousands of slaves were brought across to this place mainly from Madagascar and Mozambique.

This island ran into financial crisis due to a seven-year war between the French and the British during 1756 to 1763 and the French East India Company then governing it was on the brink of bankruptcy. As such, they decided to hand over the island back to the French state in 1765. The king of France sent Pierre Poivre to head the administration of the island who introduced cultivation of spiced plants here as well as in neighbouring areas of Bourbon and the Seychelles. The present Pamplemousses Botanical Gardens are created by him, which provide a very rich collection of spice plants and exotic trees and flowers. He was instrumental in the liberalization of trade with India after the end of monopoly of the French East India Company. As a result of that, the harbour regained a brisk activity.

The British arrived in the North of the Island on 29th November 1810 and marched towards Port Louis. After the British victory was made official by the treaty of Paris in 1814, the first British Governor was Robert Townsend Farquhar. The treaty confirmed the honourable terms arrived at between the British and the French in 1810 especially related to property, traditions, the laws, the religious practices and the languages in use in the country (It was agreed that the British will not disturb the French language in use on the Island). Further, in 1835, slavery was abolished in the colony, (Mauritius, History of Mauritius 1488-1968, 2007)

As a result of abolition of slavery, a large number of slaves who were freed, refused to work in the fields, with the result that the sugar industry and the agriculture work almost came to a standstill. As a consequence of that, the white planters had no option but to turn to British India. It is reported that hundreds of thousands of indentured labourers were brought to the island from India during the 19th century to work in the Sugarcane fields. They started arriving on a regular basis from 2nd November 1834 when the ship Atlas reached Port Louis. They were mostly of Hindu, Christian or Muslim faith and were mainly drawn from different regions of pre-partition India. Most of them spoke Hindi, Bhojpuri, Urdu, Tamil, Telugu and Marathi. From India, they mainly embarked for Mauritius from Bombay, Calcutta and Madras ports. However, most of the immigrants started from Calcutta and the Muslim immigrants were known as Calcuttya "Musulmans" or "Jolahas" (Weavers). Only a few of them came from Bengal whereas most of them were migrants from Bhojpuri belt of the states of Bihar and Uttar Pradesh. As such, Bhojpuri became the lingua franca of the indentured Indian labourers. Around the same time, a number of Indian traders mainly Muslims came from Kutch and Surat (Memons from Kutch and Surtees from Surat) in Gujarat. The Surtees constructed mosques in villages where many of them had settled and they maintained their trading accounts in Gujarati, that is, in their mother tongue.

Because of a large number of Indian traders and religious leaders of both the Hindu and Muslim faith coming to Mauritius, it led to socio-cultural development of the inhabitants of the Indian origin on the Island. A few Hindu arrived from Madras Presidency. Most of the Tamil like Sindhi traders settled in Port Louis.

Till 1839, Indian labourers were not governed by any legislation for their working conditions and they were at the mercy of their employers. Employment conditions were not conducive as those who failed to report for duty even for a day were subjected to double deductions in their wages. They were also forced to work on Sundays for which they were not paid any wage. As on 1947, people of Indian origin were 278,803 (142,457 males and 136,346 females) that is, 63.5 percent of the population. However, in 1846 their number stood at 35.5 percent of the total population (Dukhira, 2002).

In just a few years time, the Indians became the most important component of the Mauritian population, thus changing the socio-cultural composition of the island. The sugar industry developed in the 19th century further got a boost during the 20th century and sugar factories were spread across the entire island. Each sugar factory had established social activities for its employees in a decentralized manner by providing them with roads, houses, education and medical care facilities within the factory area so as to retain their inhabitation in villages around the estates. As a consequence of that, the country as a whole and the structure of the society changed and wore a new look.

Towards the late 19th century in 1860, there was a great malaria epidemic, which affected Port Louis and compelled a number of people to move to Plaines Wilhems, thereby causing the creation of towns like Curepipe, Vacoas and Rose-Hill. Further, the introduction of railways in 1864 also led to large-scale migration of the population to other regions of the island.

The 20th century was a struggle for political freedom. With the establishment of labour party in 1936, led by Sir Seewoosagur Ramgoolam, a British trained physician who

Seewoosagur Ramgoolam, a British trained physician who returned to the country after spending 12 years in England, there was mobilization of people of Indian origin to fight for the independence of the country. He was duly supported by the Muslim leaders of Indian origin who established a political output, the Committed Action Musulman (CAM) in 1959. Both these political parties entered into a pro-independence alliance. However, in 1960's a new party Parti-Mauricien Social Democrate (PMSD) headed by Gaetan Duval, a person of white origin, was opposing the independent movement because of the fear of domination of people of Indian origin. However, after the visit of Mahatma Gandhi and his emissary Manilal Doctor and the establishment of Arya Samaj and Sanatan Dharma Associations, the independent movement got intensified and with the support of the Muslim Political Outfit (CAM), the efforts of the Indo-Mauritians culminated into the Independence of Mauritius from the British Colony on 12th March, 1968. Sir Seewoosagur Ramgoolam became the first Prime Minister of the Country, during an official flag raising ceremony at Champ de Mars. He is now referred as the "Father of the Nation".

A very small segment of Mauritian population hails from China. Unlike people of Indian origin and a number of French who arrived generally as contract workers, the Chinese ancestors mostly came as free immigrants. It is reported that after 1835, the flow of immigrations from China was not allowed but due to socio-political and economic agitation in China, their number increased in Mauritius after 1840. The immigrants included sailors, traders and artisans but they had no particular occupation. However, by 1861, out of total of 1552 Chinese immigrants, 221 had settled as shopkeepers in the Districts of Port Louis and Pamplemousses whereas 92 in Plaines Wilhems. By the end of the 19th century, most Chinese who migrated to Mauritius were

Hakka; China was suffering from famine and poverty and many males moved out of their families while women continued to work in fields and took care of the elderly at home. Because of that, the Chinese immigrants at that time were predominantly male. However, more number of women from China started coming to Mauritius during the beginning of the 20th century. In 1944, the Chinese immigrants comprised of 6808 males and 4079 females and according to the Census done then, 42.44 percent of them retained Chinese nationality. By 1962, the number of those who had adopted Chinese nationality had dropped to 15.32 percent, because by that time 12176 Chinese immigrants had adopted Mauritian nationality. On arrival, they were mostly following Confucianism, Buddhism and Taoism. But later on, many of them followed Roman Catholicism. However, they did not give up their original religion and practiced it concurrently. (Dukhira, 2002).

In short, Mauritius represents an amalgam of population drawn from Europe, Africa and India. The Europeans include white planters and other settlers from France and Britain while Africans include black Creoles. The Indians are represented both by the Hindus and Muslims while the Chinese are drawn in from the Asian regions of the world.

Population

It may be mentioned right in the beginning that Mauritius attained its Republic status in 1992. As a result of that, besides the mainland island of Mauritius, the island of Rodrigues also got included as a part of its republic, along with some other smaller islands around. However, since this study is confined only to the island of Mauritius, we shall give an account of the population aspects related only to it.

As on 2006, the population of island of Mauritius is estimated to be 1.219 million of which the male population is 0.603 million whereas the females constitute 0.616 million.

The population is spread over an area of 1,8648 sq. km., with an average density of 654 persons per sq. km.

The average annual rate of increase of population during the decade of 1990-2000 is 1.10 percent. The urban-rural divide of population is 0.640 million and 0.579 million respectively. The average annual inter-censusal increase of population between 1990-2000 is 1.96 percent for urban areas and 0.51 percent for rural population. This is indicative of a trend of migration from rural to urban centres. The major urban centres included are Port Louis, Beau Bassin/ Rose-Hill, Quatre Bornes, Vacoas/Phoenix and Curepipe. The entire population of the island is distributed into nine geographical Districts namely Port Louis, Pamplemousses, Riviere du Rempart, Flacq, Grand Port, Savanne, Plaines Wilhems, Moka and Black River. The highest population is concentrated in Plaines Wilhems (03.58 millions) whereas on the lower side is Black River (60,587) (Census, 2000). There are on an average 1023 females per 1000 males. The mean age of population is 32.6 years (male 31.9; female 33.4) whereas the median age of the population is 31.0 years (male 30.3, female 30.7). The dependency ratio of population is 436.0 per 1000 population (male 426.1, female 445.8 per 1000 population as on 1st July, 2006). Further, it is reported that the Crude Birth rate is 13.8 in July 2006 while the Crude Death rate is 7.3. Even the infant mortality rate (deaths of children under 1 year of age for 1000 live births) is 13.5 while it was as high as 64.1 in 1965. However, the marriage rate (no of persons civilly married in a year per 1000 mid period population) is reported to be 10.8 in 1965 whereas in 2006 it is 18.5. It is apparent from the above data that there are more number of females than men who are dependent on the working population. Further, the sex-ratio in favour of females, should speak for better status of women in the society. Even, an increase in marriage rate may be indicative of increase in the registered marriages on the island.

The general fertility rate as on 2006 is 49.66 (that is, live births occurred per 1000 women aged 15-49 years) whereas the total fertility rate is 1.69. The age specific fertility rate is reported to be highest in the age group of 25-29 (105.9) followed by in the age group of 20-24 years (98.0) and in the age group of 30-34 years (63.5), in that order. However, an interesting observation is that it is also quite high in the age group of 15-19 years (32.5). This may be indicative of the fact that early marriage of girls is still being practiced (Mauritius. Central Statistics Office, Annual Digest of Statistics, 2007).

As per 1972, Census, the community wise distribution of population is as follows: The Hindus constituted 51.82 percent of the total population whereas Muslims had a population of 16.59 percent. The General population including whites and black Creoles was 28.66 percent of the total population while the smallest group of Sino-Mauritians (Chinese) was 2.93 percent.

However, the population by ethnicity as worked out in 1991 was 41.8 percent for Hindus (Hindi speaking and of Marathi Culture) and 9.1 percent for other Hindus belonging to Tamil and Telugu linguistic groups. The Muslims constituted 16.5 percent (Sunnis and Shias and Ahmediyas). The Chinese were reported to be 3.2 percent (Buddhists and Confucianists) while the general population including Creoles, coloured, that is, mixed and whites formed 29.4 percent of the total population (Source: Maurice 1993, p 12 as given in Dukhira, 2002).

As is apparent from the above, there is preponderance of the people of Indian origin followed by that of the general population and Chinese. Despite acculturating influence of one ethnic group over the other, each group has maintained its cultural identity.

Racial and Ethnic Composition

Racism was accepted during the colonial administration. There was discrimination shown against the coloured population and the Indians by the whites. The white despised and ridiculed the coloured people and the Indians to a very large extent. This resulted in creating a sort of complex among them and they developed hatred towards their own origin and pigmentation. They started considering the whites as their role models and to match them, they incorporated some of the values and attitudes of the whites to raise their social status. A number of efforts were made by coloured people to fight out the discrimination against them.

In order to get economic emancipation and political freedom, they launched various movements which resulted ultimately in repealing all legislations against their discrimination in civil or in military life. The Indians who came from Pondicherry during the French period got gradually integrated into the local population. They were nearly 900 of them by the end of 1831. They were free Indians and mostly belonged to Roman Catholic faith. However, they regarded themselves culturally as French but they were categorized as coloured. A number of free coloured became owners of both the sugar estates and the slaves. Some of them even opposed the liberation of slaves but the discrimination against the coloured people by the whites continued. Even in the Roman Catholic churches on the island, separate masses were organized during Easter for whites till early 1950s. Although the British respected the

French language and culture because of the treaty between the two nations, yet the English language and culture was instrumental in raising voice by the coloured community against racism of Franco-Mauritians to control the press, the Government, the Catholic church, the economy and indeed the entire country.

One can find three main races, that is, Negroid, Mongoloid and Caucasoid on the island. (The Caucasoids, however, have been sub-divided as Nordic, Alpine and Mediterranean). The Franco-Mauritians constitute the white Caucasoids and black Negroids while the Indo-Mauritians including both the Hindus and Muslims belong to Mediterranean Caucasoid racial stock. The Chinese in Mauritius possess the Mongoloid physical traits (Dukhira, 2002).

After making a succinct presentation of the racial composition in Mauritius, it may be significant to highlight the ethnic composition of the population on the island. Ethnicity is believed to be stage of socio-political evolution that preceded the democratic modern institutions. On that basis, some scholar advocated that nations of South (developing) were bound by ethnicity while that of North (developed) had evolved democratic systems, which had taken care of ethnic or regional groups to provide political stability. In the present scenario, the above proposition appears to be wrong, as ethnicity has surfaced in almost all political systems across the developed and developing worlds. Anthropologists have been stressing that ethnicity should not be viewed in the above context but may be conceived as the inherent capacity of any human society to create symbolic, linguistic and social codes. In other words, ethnicity represents a system of codes that gives meaning, identity and a sense of belongingness to distinguish one group from the other in a community or society (Arzipe, 1992). However, Giddens

(1989) defines ethnicity as cultural practices and outlooks that distinguish a given community of people on the basis of primordial types such as race, religion, kinship, language and territory. We shall discuss in brief the ethnicity observed in Mauritius on the basis of religion, caste and linguistic groups.

Religious Composition

There are four major religions pursued in Mauritius. These are Christianity, Hinduism, Islam and Buddhism. Nearly 30 percent of the population belongs to the Christianity faith. These include Franco-Mauritians, Creoles and other coloured people. The Hindus who have many sects (the two major ones being the Arya Samaj and the Sanatan Dharma) represent 52 percent of the population (this includes Bihari Hindus, Tamils, Telugus and Marathi speaking people). The Muslims who follow Islam are only 17 percent of the population but they are having several sects, the prominent among them being Shias, Sunnis and Ahmediyas, whereas only one percent of Chinese follow Buddhism and others among them are included in the category of Christianity (Simmons, 1982).

Caste Composition

In Mauritius, among the Hindus, four major caste groups as observed in India, that is, Brahmins, Kshatriyas, Vaisyas and Shudras, exist. It is considered in certain quarters that caste system is not as rigid as found in India. However, our observations confirmed that caste plays a significant role in marriage circles as well as in political arena at the time of elections. Since most of the Hindus who migrated to Mauritius came from the states of Bihar and Uttar Pradesh, all the caste groups existing in those states in India are believed to be found over here. It is reported by Carter (2000) that the first migrants from Bihar to Mauritius on their arrival declared their caste as:-

Ahir (Herdsman/ Milkman), Bania (Merchant/ Moneylender), Bedar (Soldier in Public Service), Beldar (Digger), Bhoyar (Cultivator), Bhumiyar (Land owner), Brahmin (Priest), Cahar (Carrier), Chamar (Leather worker), Dangri (Vegetable Grower), Darzi (Tailor), Dhobi (Washerman), Dosaid/ Dusadh (Village Watchman), Doni (Helper for cremation), Gosain (Religious medicant), Gowala (Milkman/cattle breeder), Hajjam (Barber), Halwai (Confectioner/Grin Parcher), Jat (Land owner/Cultivator), Julaha (Weaver), Kahar Palaquin (Bearer/Household servant), Kasai (Butcher), Kayasth (Accountant/writer/ Clerk), Kewat (Boatman/fisherman), Koiry (cultivator), Kshatriya (Warrior/Land owner), Kumhar (Potter), Kurmi (Cultivator), Lohar (Blacksmith), Mali (Gardener/Vegetable grower), Mallah (Boatman/ fisherman), Nai (Barber), Nunia (Salt Refiner/Digger), Ojha(Augur and Medium), Pasi (Toddy Drawer/Labourer), Rajput (Soldier/Land Onwer), Rangrez (Dyer), Sudh (Cultivator), Sunar (Goldsmith/ Silversmith), Teli (Oilman)

There is hardly any record available in regard to the proportion of different caste groups among the Hindus in Mauritius. However, it is observed that the largest group of Northern Indians, that is, Bihari Hindus are divided into caste-based divisions. The Brahmins are known as "Maharajs" whereas Kshatriyas are called "Babujees". Together, they constitute a small proportion of the Hindu population. The largest group of Indian Hindus belong to the Vaish caste groups or Varna and a substantial number of Ravived (Scheduled Caste) are also inhabiting the island. The majority of them have adopted the Arya Samaj sect. Besides, there are a small proportion of Tamil, Telugu and

Marathi speaking minorities who are also divided vertically along caste lines like Bihari Hindus but they want to retain their identity more as linguistic groups and keep themselves separate from the other Hindus. It is observed that the Bihari Hindus because of their numerical dominance play an important role in Mauritian politics as every Prime Minister of the country with the exception of one since independence has been a Vaish Hindu (the exception was of a Franco-Mauritian Paul Berenger, who compromised to accept the top position on power sharing basis with the Vaish Hindu)

Linguistic Groups

Language is an important aspect of one's cultural life. Usually the language spoken at home or that taught or spoken at the school is instrumental in the socialization of children. The early years of socialization through language communication imbibes in children certain set of values, attitudes, opinions, beliefs and practices that help an individual to build his or her personality in the due course of time. As indicated in population Census 2000, the language usually or most often spoken at home is Creole (70.1 percent) followed by Bhojpuri (12.1 percent), French (3.4 percent), Chinese languages (0.7 percent), Hindi (0.6 percent), English (0.3 percent), Tamil (0.3 percent), Marathi and Telugu (0.3 percent each), Urdu (0.1 percent) while 12 percent speak other language including a combination of languages. (Housing and Population Census, Mauritius, 2000).

It is apparent from the above data that Creole, which is a broken form of French and includes words from Bhojpuri, Urdu, Tamil, Telugu etc is the most spoken language for day to day use. In the post-independent era, efforts have been made by respective governments to promote Hindi, Urdu and other Indian Languages such as Marathi, Tamil, Telugu at the school as well as at the college level. Yet the predominance of Creole language is indicative of increasing influence of this language on the life style of people. This appears to have become language **1 (one)** on the island and its domination has overshadowed the other languages which subsume lower status in the hierarchy of language structure. Unfortunately, this has remained only a spoken language and despite efforts to develop a script for it, there is no substantial success achieved in this direction.

Economy

Mauritian economy has been dominated by the monocrop of sugar. Of the total land area of 186,500 hectares, nearly 46 percent is classified as agricultural land of which sugarcane cultivation alone accounts for about 41 percent (76,840 hectares). Before independence (March 1968), Mauritius had a stagnant economy. The population growth was against the increase in national Income but during the 1970s, its economy showed positive signs of growth and development. There was a record production of sugar crop and the sustained high sugar prices during that period also boosted the other sectors of development such as construction, trade and the manufacturing industries. In 1976, the per capita income at current prices was Rs. 4278. At that point of time, sugar accounted for nearly 90 percent of the total export earnings, absorbing 1/3rd of the total labour force and contributing more than 50 percent towards the Gross National Product. However, these figures need not to be taken as indicative of high level of living by the majority of population as income disparities were observed to be wide especially between the sugar planters, small planters and tenant planters. Even during that period, 60 percent of the active population above the age of 15 years was unemployed and nearly 40 percent of them, were observed to be in the age group of 15-24 years. Nearly three-fourth of the sugar proceeds accrued to twenty one sugar estates both for planting and milling operations and only one-fourth to nearly thirty one thousand owners and tenant planters.

After sugar, the next important crop grown in Mauritius is tea, which is grown over nearly 688 hectares of land area and has a production of 1567 tons. The other crops on limited scale include tobacco, maize, groundnuts, potatoes, tomatoes, other vegetables and pulses. Rice cultivation was also tried on a limited scale without affecting the sugar cane production. Even live-stock breeding was encouraged on the island and nearly 25 thousand cow keepers during the 70s were partly meeting the milk requirements of the people. However, by and large, milk products were imported. Even fishing annual catch was not enough for consumption purposes because of over-exploitation of the sea by the outsiders. To supplement agriculture, the manufacturing industries were promoted in the post-independence era. The important industrial units were that of furniture making, aluminium and plastic goods manufacturing, tuna canning, repair of ships and fertilizers. The Export-Processing Zone Act promulgated in December 1970 further boosted the start of manufacturing industries as by September 1974, as many as 9000 jobs were created in 36 industries in the field of electronics, toys, garments and diamond cutting and polishing under the Export Processing Zones (Mehta, 1981).

As of now, because of diversification in economy due to opening of it to tourism, Export Processing Zones, textile and garment industry, the GDP at basic prices is around 6064 million US dollars (199,560 Mauritian rupees) whereas the per capita GDP growth is 4.7 percent. The inflation rate as reported by Consumer Price Index (CPI) is also around 5 percent whereas the unemployment rate is around 10 percent.

Though, Mauritius has adopted market economy in principle, the daily economic life is more complex. The intervention of the state has influenced the factors affecting the product/service market. There is a strong regulation of labour laws and state intervention on companies providing public services like energy, transport, trade products such as flour and rice. However, market competition is still constrained by the rule of oligarchic families who had dominated major plantations, financial institutions, real estate, trade and telecommunications. These larger corporations are nothing but diversified off-shoots of the old sugar barons. These companies are hardly independent and are managed by the same families. There is a need to break the family ownership of these concerns and promote democratic governance of the economy.

Labour laws have been observed to hamper the effectiveness and competitiveness of such companies. Besides, there is the monopolistic pattern of the domestic Mauritian market especially related to construction, steel, beverages and detergents. We need to end the same by establishing anti-monopoly agencies. Moreover, the international trade though fairly liberalized has to encounter a number of regulation and red tapism. The banking system is comprised of a small number of operators, sometimes having dubious investors or speculators. No doubt, off-shore banking had improved the economy but a check needs to be made against money laundering. Some 900 non-banking financial institutions provide services in fund management, international arbitration and other capital market activities. No doubt, the Central bank has to provide a support function over other banks but there is an element of fraud observed even in the dominant Mauritius Commercial Bank (Bertelsmann Stiftung, 2007).

Despite economic expansion on the island over the last four decades since independence, a large proportion of people are still living below poverty line. Though, the poverty line has not been defined in Mauritius either in monetary or in non-monetary terms but based at the half median monthly household income (Mauritius household budget survey, 2006-07), the proportion of poor households below the relative poverty line has increased from 7.7 percent in 2001-02 to 8 percent in 2006-07. There is a higher proportion of households below the poverty line in rural than in the urban or semi urban areas of the island. (Mauritius, Central Statistics Office, **Economic and Social Indicators**, 2007).

The economy has already diversified and moved away from agriculture (sugar plantations and milling) and has expanded into tourism, textile and export of ready made garments, real estate, manufacturing industries, fishing, beverages, hotel industry, shopping malls and complexes, information technology but, by and large, these are dominantly owned by a small segment of the population (not more than 3 percent) who are sugar barons. In fact, the wealth of the nation is concentrated in the hands of a few families and for effective democratic governance of the economy, this needs to be deconcentrated and decentralized

Polity

As stated in the historical account, Mauritius after a long and continued struggle against the British colonist, attained independence on 12th March, 1968 (The freedom struggle was heralded by Sir Seewoosagur Ramgoolam, the chief leader of the Mauritian Labour Party and he became the first Prime Minister of the island nation. The independence movement was supported by a Comitted Action Musulman (CAM) and Independent Forward Block (IFB) while the Party Mauricien Social Democrate (PMSD) opposed it. However, after independence, Mauritius adopted the British parliamentary system of governance. The entire country was divided into 20 Constituiencies and three members from each of these were elected to form the National Assembly. There were two elected representatives from the nearby island of Rodrigues, a territory which formed the part of this nation. In order to guarantee seats for minorities on the island, a 'Best Loser' system was adopted and eight seats to the parliament were set aside for persons to be nominated to the Assembly, to constitute a total of 70 members Parliamentary body. Mauritius attained sovereign independent state within the Commonwealth and the Queen of England was its head of state. A Governor-general was appointed by Queen on the recommendation of the Prime Minister and his Cabinet colleagues acted on her behalf to administer the affairs of the country.

The New Constitution adopted by the Parliament protected fundamental human rights and the individual freedom. Besides, no citizen had to be discriminated on the basis of race, place of origin, political allegiance, colour or creed. Any amendment in the Constitution could become effective only by a majority of either $2/3^{rd}$ or $3/4^{th}$ of all M.Ps (Members of Parliament) depending upon its different sections. After independence, many political parties emerged but the two major ones, one led by French leftist Paul Berenger (Mouvement Militant Mauricien, (MMM) and the other led by Bihari Hindu, Jugnauth (Mouvement Socialiste Mauricien (MSM) played crucial role in managing the political dynamics of the nation either in alliance or in opposition with the Labour Party and smaller political formations active along ethnic lines.

However, Mauritius attained its Republic status on 12th March, 1992 and the Governor General was replaced by the President. Sir Veeraswamy Ringadoo, the former Finance

Minister of Labour Party became the first president of the Republic of Mauritius. Mauritius had either coalition or alliance politics of different political outfits to provide power structure to its citizens in a fairly peaceful and compatible manner without much upheavels and outbursts. This is indicative of the emergence of a matured political system on the island though minor abberations or incidents of political fighting between or within groups cannot be ruled out.

The Republic of Mauritius has the island of Mauritius, as well as the island of Rodrigues and other small islands as its constituents. The population of Mauritius as estimated on 2006 is about 1.2 million while that of Rodrigues is about 37,000. The other smaller islands are inhabited only by 289 persons. As mentioned earlier, the island of Mauritius is divided into urban and rural areas. The major urban centres are Port Louis, Beau Bassin/Rose-Hill, Quatre Bornes, Curepipe, Vacoas/Phoenix. The entire island is divided into nine geographical districts as stated earlier under population statistics. The election to the District Councils and Village Councils and Municipal Councils are held every 5 years as a part of the local government set-up. To the National Assembly, these are also held after every 5 years according to the Representative of People Act and the related Regulations of the People Act as provided in the Constitution. However, the District Council Elections are held indirectly as one representative of each council of the area is chosen from its members. The political structure is supported by a bureaucracy which has executive powers delegated to them by the council of Ministers in the Prime Ministers' Cabinet whereas the Judiciary system upholds the Law and order and Social Justice areas of administrations.

Social Services

It is observed that some efforts were made by the Government for the welfare of its people in the beginning of the last century. However, the social welfare measures became visible only after the 1948 elections based on adult suffrage. In 1948, the sugar industry labour welfare fund was created to promote the welfare of workers employed in sugar industry. Wage earners got organized and certain institutional changes were introduced for the welfare of the workers.

However, of various social services provided to people, three of them namely education, health including population control measures and social security, need to be highlighted in the context of Mauritius as a welfare state.

Education

In the post-independence era, the then government in power led by Labour Party, made primary education free in Government and other aided schools. In 1974, 233 such schools were providing education upto 6th standard and the student enrolment was 92 percent of the school age population. Secondary Education, which was mostly dominated by private aided and non-aided institutions, was also made free by the Government. In 1974, secondary education of 5 years duration was provided in 124 schools having sixty thousand students on roll. The pupil-teacher ratio in primary and secondary education was 26 and 32 respectively. The literacy rate then was 72.57 percent (based on the exclusion of population below 5 years of age) (Mehta, 1981).

Efforts were also made to vocationalize education and technical schools, workshops and laboratories accessible to private secondary schools and an industrial training centre, were also set-up in the country. Higher education facilities were available in the faculties of Administration, Agriculture and Industrial Technology at the University of Mauritius, established in 1965. The other important institutions opened up in the post independence period were, an Institute of Education to prepare personnel for developing the course contents, methods and teaching aids for the primary and secondary school teachers, Mahatma Gandhi Institute to emphasize Indian Culture and history and the Mauritius College of the Air, to provide courses on Radio and T.V.

Education over the years has expanded enormously on the island. By 2006, there are about 1055 pre-primary schools having an enrolment of 35,786 students and a teaching staff of 2453. The sex-wise distribution of students in these schools is nearly equal. Besides, the average number of pupils per teacher works out to be 15. As on March 2007, 276 schools provide primary education on the island. The majority of the schools are run by the Government (210), 51 by Roman Catholic Education Authority, 2 by the Hindu Education Authority and other 17 are private non-aided schools. Nearly 74 percent of the primary school population was enrolled in Government schools while the remaining was in private aided and non-aided schools. Boys represented 51 percent of the primary school population while girls constituted 49 percent. The pupil-teacher ratio in primary school works out to be 28. In the certificate of primary education examination, it was observed that in 2006, the girls were more successful than the boys, having respective pass rates of 74 percent and 62 percent. There are as many as 181 schools providing secondary education on the island, mostly run by private aided and non-aided agencies (116) while the rest are administered by the state. Among the students, 52 percent are girls and 48 percent are boys. Nearly 38 percent of the students are in state schools while 62 percent are in private aided and unaided schools. Those preparing for Cambridge School Certificate in 2006 had an overall pass percentage of 78.9 whereas in respect of the Cambridge Higher School Certificate examination, the overall pass percentage was 79.3. In both these examinations, the females seem to be showing better results. In regard to tertiary education, there appears an increase of 15.1 percent enrolment (including the part time and full-time students) as on December 2006 in comparison to December 2005. The majority of students were enrolled in tertiary education locally in both public funded institutions (47 percent) and private institutions (28 percent) while 25 percent of the students were enrolled in tertiary education overseas. (Mauritiuis, Central Statistics Office, **Education Statistics**, 2007).

In addition to the expansion of education as stated above in the island of Mauritius, as on March 2006, there are 147 schools offering free vocational education, covering a student population of 9903 (6095 males and 3808 females) and a teaching staff of 651, thereby providing a pupil/teacher ratio of 15. Besides, the University of Mauritius provides higher education by offering courses (M.Phil/Ph.D., M.A. degree, diploma/degree, diploma and certificate) in the Faculties of Agriculture, Engineering, Law and Management, Science and Social Studies and Humanities. The total enrolment of students in all the Faculties in 2006-07 is 7370.

The technical institute such as University of Technology in Mauritius in 2006-07 has an enrolment of 352 students in School of Business Informatics and Software Engineering while 1268 in the Public Sector Policy and Management. The Mauritius Institute of Health offering Post-graduate Medical studies (general surgery, psychiatry, cardiology, orthopaedic surgery, internal medicine, paediatrics and forensic medicine) has a total enrolment of 24 students (19 males and 5 females) in the year 2006-07. The Mauritius Institute of Education offering various courses (Master degree in education, post–graduate certificate in education,

Bachelor in Education, Diploma, Advanced Certificate and teachers certificate) has an enrolment of 3106 students (1348 males and 1758 females). This appears significant as more number of females are opting for educational field. The Mahatma Gandhi Institute offers post-graduate course in M.A. (Hons) Hindi degree, B.A. (Hons.) in Hindi, Urdu, Indian philosophy, Fine Arts, Mauritian studies, Fine Arts with education, Hindi, Urdu, Marathi, Telugu and Tamil with education, Performing Arts such as Sitar, Bharatnatyam and vocal music, diploma, degree in fine arts, diploma in above disciplines, advance certificate in Indian music and dance, certificate in Telugu and Indian music and dance. As on 2005-2006, it has an enrolment of 3087 students (1123 males and 1964 females).

In view of the above expansion of education on the island, the total government expenditure for the financial year 2007-08 is Rs. 61544 million out of which Rs. 7812 million (13 percent) has been allocated to education. On further breakdown, 51 percent is for secondary education, 25 percent for primary education, 11 percent for post secondary education. 4 percent for technical and vocational education, 2 percent for pre-primary education and the remaining 7 percent includes other expenses. No doubt, the educational input of such a great magnitude is necessary to make Mauritius a knowledge based society, but there is need for greater inputs in specialized professional courses such as management, information technology, medicine, legal studies and engineering technology to accelerate and sustain the development process on the island.

Health and Population

In the pre-independence period because of the inhuman conditions of work for labourers on the farms, a Commission was appointed on October 1943 as recommended by Browne

Report. This report had described the labour engaged in plantation work as poorly paid, undernourished, sick and with limited output of work. The Commission, headed by Col. Moody emphasized on the improvement in the standard of life and quality of the population by encouraging collective bargaining, general welfare and health, housing and sanitation, hospitals and the human factor. In the subsequent period and in the post-independent era, through a network of hospitals and dispensaries, the government provided free medical services to the entire population. By 1974, there were six general and four specialized hospitals for the public. The bed availability in the hospitals improved and the doctor-bed ratio increased from 5 to 8 per 100 beds. Mobile dispensaries also operated in the rural areas. Besides, immunization and family planning services were also provided on certain days in a week at the Social Welfare Centres in the villages.

Over the years, there has been a widespread of health services across the island. As on 31st December 2006, there are 5 regional hospitals, 3 district hospitals, 4 specialized hospitals covering psychiatry, chest, eye and ENT treatments. Besides, there is one cardiac centre, two medi-clinics, 27 Area Health Centres and 126 Community Health Centres. In addition, there are 3 Family Health Service centres, providing only maternal and child health and family planning services. There are also 13 private dispensaries located on sugar estates and one mobile dispensary. Besides, there are 50 dental clinics including oral surgery and orthodontics, one social hygiene, 12 private and 2 public mobile dental clinics. To meet these services, there are 856 government doctors, out of which 253 are Specialists while as many as 544 doctors do private practice (in all 1400 doctors), 56 Government engaged dentists and 117 private dentists. The number of pharmacists engaged in government services is 22 while the majority of pharmacists (269) operate in the private sector. However, there are 2905 qualified nurses and mid-wives working in the government sector while only a small number (165) is engaged in the private sector. The most common contagious or communicable diseases as reported in 2006 are HIV/AIDS (555 cases), food poisoning (78 cases), gonorrhea (41 cases), malaria (38 cases), syphilis (35 cases) and tuberculosis (103 cases)

The life expectancy at birth in 2004 is reported to be 72 years (69 for males and 75 for females). The under 5 mortality per 1000 live births has also been brought down to 15 (17 for males and 14 for females). The maternal mortality per lakh live birth is also reported to be 24. The infant mortality rate per 1000 live births has also been brought down to 12. The most common causes of death among children under 5 years of age are pneumonia and injuries whereas the diseases causing death among the adult population are TB, cardio-vascular diseases, cancer, injuries and other communicable and non-communicable diseases. Neo-natal mortality is high (66 percent) among both the sexes. Diabetes is emerging as a serious health problem on the island besides heart and cerebro-vascular diseases. Besides, tuberculosis has a prevalence of 135 morbidity rate per one lakh population whereas its incidence among both sexes in 2004 was reported to be 64 per one lakh population. The behaviour and environmental risk factors identified causing health hazards among adults are obesity (more among females than males) tobacco use and alcoholism etc. However, there is total coverage of people's access to improved water sources, improved sanitation both in urban and rural areas (Mauritius, Central Statistics Office, Annual Digest of Statistics, 2006-07). Country Health System, Fact Sheet, 2006, Mauritius, World Health Statistics, 2006).

In view of the above growth and development of health and family welfare services across the island, one is convinced of the efforts of the state machinery to provide quality services to its population. The annual growth rate has been brought down to 0.9 percent between the years 1995 and 2004. The total fertility rate per woman is also around 2 whereas the adolescent fertility proportion is reported to be around 9.6 percent. No doubt, the mortality rate has been brought down to 7.3, but the morbidity data appear to be on the higher side as revealed by heavy rush in hospitals and dispensaries observed during our personal visits to these places. This may necessitate further expansion of health care services especially for the emerging health problems like diabetes, respiratory diseases, cardio-vascular diseases, cerebro-vascular diseases and other neo-natal diseases affecting the health of the infants. There is a need to check environmental health hazards such as respiratory diseases due to increasing vehicular emissions as the density of vehicles is becoming threatening on the island. This must be given a priority because if not checked adequately, it will give rise to respiratory diseases. Tourism, being a developed industry must take care of the environmental pollution through the spread of garbage and solid waste material. Even water pollution is a serious problem that needs rapt attention by the government authorities as well as by NGOs to combat the menace of new health hazards. The redeeming feature is that through family planning measures, the population growth has been checked or controlled within desirable limits but an increase in poverty ratio is vulnerable to cause further health hazards.

Social Security

Mauritius embraced democracy and as an extension of it adopted a welfare policy for the benefit of its people.

A number of public services and facilities are enjoyed by certain sections of the Mauritian population. The most significant measures of welfare in Mauritius are health and education (as discussed above and both are provided free), social security benefits and housing, pensions, basic retirement benefits, subsidized rice and flour etc. Even before independence in 1948, the sugar industry labour welfare fund was created to promote the welfare of workers employed in the sugar industry. A scheme for family allowance to families having 3 or more children under the age of 14 and whose income did not exceed Rs. 225/- a month, was introduced in 1962. In July 1978, the rate of payment to each family covered under the scheme was Rs. 50 a month and nearly 40,000 families were benefiting from the scheme. Another scheme introduced by the government entitled persons over the age of sixty and not liable to pay income tax and all blind persons over the age of 18, to a state pension of Rs. 100 a month. Further, nearly 30,000 persons with inadequate income received outdoor relief averaging around Rs. 60 a month. A welfare scheme was introduced for widows as well, who were entitled to a monthly allowance of Rs. 100 (Mehta, 1981).

As from the July 2000, the Labour Party in power raised the old age pension for the senior citizens (all those aged 60 to 89, 90 to 99 and above 100 years are being given Rs. 1500, Rs. 5725 and Rs 6600 respectively per month.) Allowance granted to the sick, the handicapped, widows and orphans have also been increased keeping in view the consumer price index and the tripartite negotiations held annually since July 2001. Provisions for these beneficiaries and old age pensioners were raised from Rs. 3.7 billion to Rs. 4.1 billion in the 2002-03 budget (Dukhira, 2002)

The social benefits provided to the people of Mauritius as well as to the inhabitants of Rodrigues include social aid, indoor relief to persons, infirmaries, orphanages, retirement pension and child's allowance including basic pension and contributory pension, widow's pension and child's allowance including basic and contributory pension, orphan's pension and guardian allowance including basic and contribution pension, invalidity pension and child's allowance including basic and contributory pension, inmates allowance to persons in infirmaries and orphanages and Brown Sequard Hospital, industrial injury benefit, lump sum payment to ex-sugar industry, provident fund members and unemployment hardship relief (Mauritius, Central Statistics Office, Annual Digest of Statistics, 2006-07).

A large number of social security measures provided to various sections of society in a welfare state like Mauritius, is a positive indication of granting equity, justice and poverty alleviation under the democratic governance. These measures are being provided by Central as well as local authorities besides voluntary, parastatal, religious or non-denominational organizations and by a few philanthropic individuals.

The profile of Mauritius as presented in the foregoing pages clearly brings out that the nation-state through its democratic governance has encouraged liberal and to a certain extent, participatory democracy, diversified the economic activities, laid foundation for bureaucratic and financial institutions and expanded social services such as education, health and other welfare activities to contain its population within reasonable limits.

References

Arzipe, Lourdes (1992), "Ethnicity, Nations and Culture", *Development*, 4, pp. 6-8 (Rome, Journal of Society for International Development),

Bertelsmann Stiftung, BTI 2008 (2007), *Mauritius Country Report*, Gutersloh, Bertelsmann, Stiftung.

Carter, Marina (2000), *Across The Kala Pahani: The Bihari Presence in Mauritius,* Mauritius, Centre for Research on Indian Ocean Societies, January, p. 52.

Dukhira, Chit (2002), *History of Mauritius, Experiments in Democrracy*, Mauritius, Quatre-Bornes, 5, Avenue des, Orchidees.

Gidden, Anthony (1989), *Sociology*, Cambridge, Polity Press.

Mehta, S.R. (1981), *Social Development in Mauritius: A study on Rural Modernization in an Island Community*, New Delhi, Wiley Eastern, Ltd.

Mauritius, (2007), *"History of Mauritius 1488-1968"*, Teleservices (Directory).

Mauritius, Central Statistics Office (2000), *Housing and Population Census*, (Ministry of Finance and Economic Development, Port Louis).

Mauritius, Central Statistics Office (2007), *Economic and Social Indicators*, (Ministry of Finance and Economic Development, Port Louis).

Mauritius, Central Statistics Office (2007), *Education Statistics*, (Ministry of Finance and Economic Development, Port Louis)

Mauritius, Central Statistics Office (2007), *Annual Digest of Statistics 2006*, Vol. 51, (Ministry of Finance and Economic Development, Port Louis).

Mauritius, World Health Statistics (2006) *Country Health System, Fact Sheet*,http://wwww.who.int/whosis/en/.

Simmons, A.S. (1982), *Modern Mauritius, The Politics of Decolonization*, Bloomington, Indiana University Press.

3

Economic Transformation: Causes for and Consequences of an Economic "Miracle"

Development Paradigms

The traditional paradigm advocated by economists is based on the concept of "economic man" which emphasizes on the goal of maximum consumption of goods and services with minimum efforts. In it, output has been considered as a function of the quantity and quality of labour, the kind of capital, the amount of land and other natural resources, the kind of entrepreneurship and the kind of technology. It is thought that as development proceeds, the capitalist will reinvest and will employ more workers. This should help in further redistribution of income to a larger segment of population. In other words, the income will trickle down. So, this is "grow now, trickle later approach". This growth strategy has failed to tackle the problems of unemployment, income inequalities, regional disparities, poverty, malnutrition and illiteracy in the developing nations, which have been subjected to the yoke of colonialism for centuries by the dominant developed nations. After getting aware of the limitations inherent in this paradigm, it was thought best by this school of economists to modify their strategy and suggest means that should help the developing nations to raise their standard of living to a minimum decent level in consistence with their own resources and with their own values. Basic human needs were to be given priority over the demand items of luxury. Production and distribution was thought to be pursued simultaneously and the poor had to be provided with means so as to realize their needs. Besides, there ought to be a judicious mix of capital and labour for a maximum return on labour rather than on capital through an appropriate use of technology. Rural Development in these nations had to be a priority, with emphasis on agriculture, agro-based industry, self-reliance, and local leadership, medical care, housing and education, to tackle the acute problem of poverty. It is here that the development strategy got separated from the growth as it advocated "Growth with Social Justice" as one of the main goals of development.

The second dominant paradigm of development is the legacy of political economists who advocate liberation at two levels as the main goal of development. The first level liberation has to be attained within the developing country so as to provide every one with basic needs, meaningful work, conducive environment for having satisfying relationships with their fellow human beings and healthy environment for living, to have a society based on equality and in consistence with people's values. Further, the developing nations must liberate themselves from the "dependency" syndrome of the rich, developed nations. They want to treat development from a historical perspective and conceive it in a holistic sense wherein societal institutions such as social, political, religious and economic must be compatible with each other in its entire process. Stress is laid on social ownership, centralized planning for allocation of resources such as land, labour and capital to direct social surplus into productive investments to meet people's basic needs especially in the rural areas by adopting social revolution as a sort of precondition for development. Facilities and industry must be taken to the villages to stop migrations to the urban or city centres. Further, elites should be replaced by committed people to do the tasks and bureaucrats within the system should work at the level where they can meet their needs to make development a dynamic process (Weaver, 1975) (This model draws much of its strategy from the Chinese model of development).

Nothwithstanding the relevance of the above dominant paradigms of development, over the years, it has been realized that both the capitalist and the socialist paradigms of development, instead of tackling the problems of poverty, unemployment and income disparities have led to population growth, health and environmental hazards, malnutrition, child labour, delinquency, growth of slums, social tensions and agrarian unrest, ethnic rifts and strifes, labourers' agitations and a host of other social evils such as dowry, divorce, drug addiction, alcoholism, prostitution besides exploitation, oppression and discrimination of backward classes by the upper class, and corruption in the developing nations (Mehta, 1999).

However, we need to move towards a good society, which should be without strains and disruptions as envisaged by social theory. On one hand, conservative thinking is for having some kind of neo-traditional social and cultural integration to attain social tranquility because modernity has caused tension in a society while on the other, radical theory blames capitalism and advocates socialism as an antidote to social disruption or strife. It is argued that both these theories are far from reality, as any kind of society (capitalist or socialist) will generate some tensions and crises in it, mainly because of scarcity of resources and motives of the people to have maximum appropriation of the same for a better standard of living. Tensions created in the development process need to be resolved by evolving mechanisms to maintain the integrity and conformity of the civil society and that perhaps is the test for moving towards a good society (Jaffery, 1990).

The majority of the societies or new nations have opted now for democratic governance and are moving towards a market economy, however, imperfect these dimensions may be there for their growth and development. However, apart from the production factors of land, labour, capital, entrepreneurship and technology (the last two factors are acquiring a lead over the others in the market economy) for development of a new nation or a developing society, we cannot ignore the geographical location, and other associated geographical parameters such as climatic zone, availability of raw materials for production of goods, and work ethic of people etc. Even, the historical circumstances of the people in a given territory as to "how they got where they are" in the entire development process especially for a long colonized nation like Mauritius, need to be examined to understand the dynamics of a growing economy which by and large, has been insulated from the outside world, yet establishing its internal mechanisms to have visible linkages with the external systems for its sustainable development.

It is recognized now that economic growth rate has some relationship with the coastal, tropical and temperate climates; we do know that tropical countries have a lower growth rate than the non-tropical ones. The majority of the countries in the tropical zone are poor because of the burden of diseases and constraints on agricultural productivity.

On the other side, nearly all countries in the mid and high altitudes are rich. It is also observed that the coastal countries have a higher income than the land-locked ones. Besides, countries having bulk of population in coastal areas, having access to oceans or ocean-navigable rivers, grow at a faster rate than those having large interior population (Gallup, Sachs and Mellinger, 1999 as quoted by Nath and Madhoo, 2008). Also, geographical remoteness also affects growth adversely because of increased transport costs involved in international trade (Limao and Venables 2001 as quoted by Nath and Madhoo, 2008).

In view of the above, the economic growth of Mauritius is bound to be affected by its size, location and climate. Small size of the island (60 kilometres by 40 kilometres) compelled Mauritius to opt for the external trade because of limited domestic market. Small size may even restrict export markets because of limited competition in the domestic front for improving international competitiveness but this has not acted as a hurdle for the export-oriented firms in Mauritius. The sub-tropical climate and rich volcanic soil of Mauritius is favourable for diversified agriculture. Besides, sugarcane plantation can be easily done by one time seed operation from which reaping of crop can be obtained for 5 to 7 times, this being a "sick" crop. The earlier settlers in Mauritius, despite abandoning sugarcane plantations initially, reverted back to its cultivation on their second occupancy. However, Mauritius falls into a strong cyclonic belt and is subjected to serious cyclonic outbursts affecting domestic agriculture. But, because of mountainous terrain, regional climatic variations exist and there are a variety of sub-climates experienced. Even the water supply on the island depends on rainfall, often brought by clouds accompanied with the rain. It is observed that during 1950-2000, 4 to 5 cyclones, especially cyclone Hollanda in 1954 had devastating effects on agricultural growth and infrastructure. Mauritius, despite being insulated from any direct contact with the neighbouring nations, was still an active supporter of regional trade integration to expand its economic space. In the absence of mineral natural resources and its vulnerability to natural hazards because of uncertain climatic weather conditions, the growth prospects become bleak. However, nature has favoured Mauritius with extraordinary beaches, extensive marine resources and beautiful landscape, attracting tourists from the rest of the world and making international tourism as an important sector in the process of economic transformation (Nath and Madhoo, 2008).

In addition to geographical context for economic growth, we need also to examine the historical circumstances contributing towards that end. Mauritius was uninhabited until the beginning of the 17th century when the Dutch brought slaves and convicts from their settlements in India and South-East Asia. They had to leave after a lapse of few years because of the attacks by the pirates and the island was mainly run by them. It was during French colonial period (1721 to 1810) that this island got established as a strategic *entrepot* on the Indian Ocean trade route. Indians played a key role in the development of this French colony as they were brought as workers, convicts, servants and even slaves. However, it was after the British takeover of the island, that it was transformed from a port of call into a thriving sugar exporter. As a result of that ,the demand for Indian labour increased considerably. By the end of 19th century, Mauritius became the premier exporter of sugar for the British regime. Besides black slaves brought from Mozambique and Madagascar, (Slavery was abolished between 1835 and 1839) people of the Indian origin (Both the Hindus and Muslims) were the dominant ethnic groups who contributed significantly to the economic development of this island nation.

Apart from convicts and indentured workers brought from India by the British, they also had a large number of Europeans and Indian troops along with them on arrival. Besides, a number of officials and assistants accompanied them to manage the civil government in the event of any successful conquest. Indians were considered trusted staff, and because of that, Veliavel Annasamy came from India to take up the position of a clerk in British administration. He established good relationships with the British Colonial elites and became a part-owner with Charles Telfair, of a sugar estate in 1822. Another Tamil merchant Rama Tiroumoudy, also became a part-owner of estate Bon Espoir. They were picked up by the British mainly because they could neither communicate nor trust the Francophone Creole inhabitants. It is also reported that the members of the existing Indian community, signed an oath of allegiance to the British and took jobs in the new government. Also Ratungee Bickagee, a Parsi merchant, after the British take over, seized the opportunities offered in the new colonial set up. He engaged himself in the lucrative business of importing goods from India, acting partly as a shipping agent and also investing his profits in the land and the shining sugar industry.

By becoming estate owners, the migrants were following the pursuits of South Indian traders who had begun to move into the domain of agriculture as large landowners. Established Tamil and Parsi merchants encouraged their co-religionists to settle on the island. The economic advancement of Mauritius by 1840s because of the concerted efforts of indentured labourers, had started attracting the attention of Gujarati traders, mostly Muslims and like other Indians, they settled in specific areas of capital (Port Louis). Subsequently, they established business interests in the transportation of Indian migrants, food and textile imports and money lending and real estate business etc. They also moved into land ownership, when sugar export to India reached its peak in 1910. However, many of the Tamil merchants moved on to South Africa when indentured Indian immigration to Natal was opened. It is reported that the Indian community in the colony whether ex-indentured labourer or merchant, because of the acquisition of wealth and land, attained prestige and social status (Marin in Lal, 2007).

In the above backdrop, one thing stands out, that despite adverse historical circumstances, some individuals because of their achievement motivation, entrepreneurial aptitude and hard working nature could realize their dreams of being wealthy and prosperous by cooperating with rather than antagonising the colonial regime. The tolerance as a part of Indian value system has always stood the test of time and cultural pluralism has bestowed upon the people of Indian origin, a sustained effort towards progress of this island community or society.

Economic Transformation

Pre-Independence Scenario

Till independence in 1968, Mauritian economy was dominated by the mono crop of sugar cane. Capital and land were provided by French and British colonists while the labour component of the production process was mainly contributed by immigrants from Africa (slaves from Mozambique and Madagascar) and Asia (convicts, indentured workers and artisans mainly from French part of India and the British India) Technology for sugar production from cane and the entrepreneurial skills required for management and marketing of the produce, were also provided by the colonists. In fact, the labour cost of the sugar production was almost negligible while the sugar output was surplus enough to be marketed across the other parts of the world with large profits out of the international trade. In fact, the pre-independence economic scenario of Mauritius was marked by surplus labour, lack of natural resources, high commodity trade dependence (sugar), distance from present day-sea lanes resulting in high transport costs, a small domestic market, and a division of population on ethnic and religious lines. Further, its tropical climate was vulnerable for a high exposure of diseases, causing labour unproductivity. (Nath and Madhoo, 2008).

In short, the economic situation before the independence of Mauritius was that of exploitation, oppression and discrimination of the indentured labourers, convicts and slaves brought in from Africa and Asia for sugarcane cultivations. African Creoles brought as slaves from Madagascar and Mozambique were forced to work on sugar estates but after the abolition of slavery (1835 to 1839), many of them ran away and moved on to the sea sides where they built up their villages and engaged themselves in fishing occupation. Even now, there are more number of village settlements of African black Creoles on the sea-sides. Most of the Hindus who worked as indentured labourers on the sugar estates established their settlements or villages around the estates. Muslims who were brought as labourers moved on to the occupation of contractor or a *Baiyan,* that is, a middleman in the fishing business, whereas Muslim traders, mainly Gujaratis, concentrated in specific areas in urban or city centres. Chinese, who constituted a small population of the population were in trading and mostly they owned the corner shops in town and city centres, selling grocery and other consumer goods, A handful of white settlers, say 8 to 12 families, were owning or are still owning the sugar estates. They were providing entrepreneurial expertise and technology to manage as many as 21 sugar estates (20 in the private and one in government sector at the time, the data were collected by Mehta for his study (1981)). They do not constitute more than 3 percent of the total population. However, they were assisted by the middle level managerial staff who were of their religious faith (Christianity) and were mostly *mulattos* (different shades of white because of mixed breeding). However, the labour in the estates was mostly of people belonging to Indo-Mauritian stock, especially the Hindus though some Muslims also worked in agriculture. Many of the Indians who showed loyalty and allegiance to the colonists were upgraded to the status of "Sirdars" or contractors who assisted them in bringing more migrant labourers from India, through embarkment, from the port of Bombay or Calcutta (those who embarked from the port of Bombay are called Bombaias and those from that of Calcutta, are known as Calcuttyas).

The "Sirdars" or labour supervisors provided some kind of social and economic mobility. They were paid higher wages than ordinary labourers and mainly supplemented their income by shopkeeping business and money lending. By acting as intermediaries between European settlers and the Indian labour force, they gained through the process of engaging new persons from overseas, looking after reengagements, and brokering labour disputes and agreements. This suited the Europeans as the recruitment was done through the commercial contractors, as they brought persons of their own ethnic groups to an estate from the places of their own residence. With the passage of time, Indians moved off the estates and shifted to villages developed around them. The job contractors acquired further boost in their socio-economic status, as they became the employers of the Indians rather than that of plantation owners. This economic system also was in the interest of the European estate owners as they could save on the overhead expenditures accrued earlier by paying lump-sum money to the job contractors for hiring the labour. In fact, they paid wages, to the labourers and in turn ensured their availability for plantation. This way ,they could also regulate their employment. It is reported that the elite 'sirdars' and contractors, who rose from the ranks of indentured labourers became rich further by the major land transactions during the last quarter of the 19th century.

Popularly known as grand *Morcellement* policy or parcelling of lands, it became a landmark breakthrough for the *"sirdars"* and contractors to acquire or own agricultural lands with the help and support of wealthy Indians. Besides, many Indian immigrants could acquire major tracts of scrub and marginalized cane fields. Because of worldwide depression in sugar prices during that period, the white owners were compelled to sell off or subdivide their property. Enterprising *"sirdars"* and contractors, with some capital of their own, joined hands with the Indian merchants to make collective land purchases. They, in turn, divided these into smaller parts and sold them to ex-indentured labourers who became later on, owner and tenant cultivators of the cane fields. It is reported that some Indian immigrants, for example, Ramtohul became a sugar estate owner by purchasing the plantation of Mon Choix for Sp. $ 49,000 in June 1870, after making cash down payment of Sp $ 10,000. This ex-indentured Indian was the first to acquire this elevated position. (Marin in Lal, 2007).

Till independence, Mauritius had the typical plantation economy and its mono-crop of sugar, characterized by large-scale enterprises, was owned and managed by European white settlers. In fact, the capital investment and its return was concentrated in a few hands (of the 21 sugar estates, having sophisticated sugar mills, as many as 20 were being managed in the private sector while only one was operating in the public sector that too being managed by a white person). Of the total land area, more than half has been classified as agricultural land, of which sugar cane cultivation alone accounted for around 90 percent. It is reported that by 1974, out of total area under sugar, nearly 56 percent was cultivated by 21 sugar estates wherein 44 percent was cultivated by 29,539 owner planters and 1512 *metayers* (tenant) cultivators who acquired land due to policy of *Morcellement* having land holding of less than 5 arpents. (Arpent is a French measure for land-holding, which is slightly more than an acre). Even the average cane yields per arpent in the case of mill planters was observed to be three times more than that of owner-tenant planters. (Mauritius Economic Review, 1976, Mehta, 1981, 1989).

In the pre-independence period, Mauritius had a stagnant economy. Population growth was further observed to be a drag on national income. A prognosis was made on the economy of Mauritius by James Meade in 1961. (He was a recipient of the Nobel prize in Economics). He predicted that due to country's heavy dependence on one crop that is, sugar, as well as vulnerability to terms of trade shocks, rapid population growth, and potentiality of ethnic tensions, the development prospects were bleak. Besides, the country had a tropical climate and was far away from world markets than most African nations. As such, the growth chances were meagre and the outlook for peaceful development was far-fetched and poor. However, Meade was famously proved wrong by the history in the post independent era which ushered in economic "miracle" that signalled progress and prosperity in the country in comparison with the other countries in the African region. (Meade, 1961, Mauritius Economic Report on Africa, 2003).

Social relations among people are often influenced by occupational work setting as in a multiethnic community, occupational specialization gets centred around the ethnic group to which persons belong. There appeared a greater interaction within an ethnic group than between them mainly because of food habits and language communication facility, though work and market situation provided them opportunity to interact and share their cultural ethos and codes with one another. In essence, the pre-independence scenario in Mauritius was that of different ethnic groups living side-by-side, without fully mixing but mingling to eke out their existence in order to realize their basic survival needs. It was more of a panorama of a community of communities, having distinct cultural identities exhibited through institutional specificities fostering or promoting relationships between them along primordial ties such as sex, age, kinship-family networks, caste, religion, language etc. The population on the island was in fact, characterized more by cultural and social pluralism than beset as a Plural Society.

However, the scenario changed after the independence of the nation and a new script was written. An economy which was dominated during 1960s by the mono-crop of sugar as a commodity for bulk of its income, employment, export revenue, is now moving into a well developed manufacturing sector and fast expanding service sectors such as tourism, financial services, off shore services, free port and information technology (Mehta, P 2006).

Economic Development : Post Independent Diversification and Pinnacle of Economic "Miracle"

Development as a concept has encountered many changes in its connotation. It is no longer conceived now, only in terms of growth but is considered as "Growth plus Social Change". This conception has brought in the non-economic parameters to the forefront. Of late, the economists have realized that without changes in the social and cultural aspects of people in a given population, circumscribed by territorial region, it is not possible to have growth. It was realized that though initially for nearly two decades or so, the economic growth strategies and modernization paradigms showed some promise for the developing nations but subsequently these proved disastrous. It was felt that by 1980, these "new" nations were forty five times poorer than the industrialized nations. Basic human need approach, emphasising on food, shelter, and health care and education was thought suitable for achieving the goal of development. A participatory approach built in the system to mobilize labour, women, children and making development environment friendly to reduce or limit the over exploitation and over exhaustion of natural resources so that the future generations of people were not affected adversely, was suggested.

Apart from development of a nation being eco-friendly, social relations are basic to the perpetuation of a community or society by promoting group cohesiveness, social solidarity and cooperation and harmony, by simultaneously taking care of the existing conflicts, tensions and dissensions in social life for an integrated social life through a negotiated set of understanding among people to build up confidence, trust and integration. Further, social arrangements are also essential for the production process as without capital formation, development may not be possible. However, the production of goods and services need to be in consistence with the needs of the people as in nations, where needs give rise to demands, false modernization effects become visible (Mehta, 1981). We find increased income disparities, concentration of wealth in a few hands and a large segment of population getting impoverished. This is where development with social justice and equity including gender equity, needs to be pronounced. In short, the main aim of development should be to build up a new social order based on material and moral dimensions through transformation of Men and Societies, failing that development will tend to be mal-development for any society (Mehta, 1999).

In the capitalist model of development, which the majority of developing nations have adopted along with democratic governance, the moral fabric of their societies is on the decline and the material life is on the rise. In Mauritius, though the struggle for independence led by Sir Seewoosagur Ramgoolam under the banner of Fabian Socialist Labour Party culminated in the freedom of the country in 1968, yet the socialist ideas, soon after, were replaced by capitalist market forces and are continuing till now with some patchwork of welfare schemes to contain dissensions or tensions of the dis-priviledged and discriminated groups. The development process turned to be lop sided and because of wrong priorities and faulty implementation of projects and schemes, there was exclusive rather than inclusive development of people on this island-nation. Socialism, as an ideology of labour party was good to gain freedom from Britain but the capitalist model of development was so entrenched in the economy of the country by the regime of the colonists through the network of sugar-estate and sugar mills, that its riddance as a strategy of development was not an easy possibility.

The hold of colonists through the sugar estates on the labour force was absolute as without cheap labour on the estates, these would not have been cost-effective. Maximum profits from sugar sales were appropriated by these sugar-magnets while spending a part of surplus money in providing the village settlements in and around the estates with infra-structural facilities like road, connectivity, electricity, water, education and health care, "an end of the year bonus" to supplement their income as an incentive and covering them under the welfare and pension schemes. In short, it was a sort of mix up of capitalist model of development with welfare economics as an antidote to increased income disparities among the different groups.

This legacy of British regime was also carried forward by the new political setting that formed governments through an electoral process legitimised by the parliamentary system of governance. During the last four decades of independence of the society practically all through, it has been a coalition political structure that dominated its political scenario. As such, the economy of the country has witnessed highs and lows and has passed through many phases and stages of growth in different sectors such as agriculture, industry, tourism and social services such as education, health care and population control. Growth is necessary but not a sufficient condition of development. We also need to examine the income disparities, regional imbalances, employment status, incidence of poverty, price rise of essential goods and services and social and economic disparities among different ethnic groups in a cultural and social plural society or community.

Before we take up the specific economic issues, it would be apt to discuss the economic development of this nation-state in different phases. Though, Meade (1961) had pointed a gloomy picture for the Mauritian economy, due to colonial legacy and prevailing tropical climate conditions, and had recommended import-substitution industrialization policy and welfare assistance from overseas for its growth, yet the Mauritian economic "miracle" is mainly driven almost exclusively by Export Processing Zones (EPZs), Foreign Direct Investment (FDI) and Cheap labour (Romer, 1992, Rodrik, 1999 as quoted by Nath and Madhoo, 2008).

The export oriented manufacturing in Mauritius further got a boost because of the international political economy factor providing it preferential access to developed country markets and the substantial participation of local investors. It is observed that the Mauritian success story is to be understood in terms of "improved income distribution and shared growth". Because of aggressive state policy to exploit sugar preferences in European markets, Mauritius could generate substantial surplus from it to invest in other sectors of economy. Even EPZs policy helped in decentralizing the concentration of benefits by providing regional diversification of production and employment. Coalitional politics having a strong presence of Indo-Mauritians in the management of political affairs of the nation, provided a wide distribution of growth process by appropriating a substantial part of sugar surplus that used to accrue earlier largely to Franco-Mauritian economic elites, mainly by having a large relatively well-paid civil service (predominantly, of Indian origin) and a generous system of social security in the form of old-age pensions (Nath and Madhoo, 2008). The other significant factor that could be counted for economic growth of this country in the post-independent era is the visionary outlook of the Prime Minister Sir Seewoosagur Ramgoolam who laid the foundation of a good educational system across the different regions in the island to prepare individuals from various ethnic groups to manage adequately the affairs in the future through appropriate knowledge and skills. Providing health care network across the island was another significant factor in raising the productivity of labour force. Free education and health care must have remained a burden on the country's economy but this was a long-term investment for the realization of benefits at a later period.

The first growth phase in the Mauritian economy (1960-70) was that of growth with import substitution strategy. It was marked by low growth rate, conservative management and rising unemployment resulting into an average real growth rate of 0.7 percent and an estimated unemployment rate of more than 20 percent and that too among mostly young, educated school leavers. With the establishment of the Development Bank of Mauritius in 1964 to support the industrial policy formulated in 1963, the dependence on agriculture especially sugar was to be reduced by establishing food processing, beverages, cosmetics, fertilizers, footwear, furniture and paints industries to meet local needs. This was followed by take off growth phase from 1971 to 1977 wherein a greater role was given to the private sector and foreign investors through the establishment of Mauritius Export Processing Zone by the government to create job opportunities and provide impetus to import substitution and export oriented industries. By 1974, as many as 102 industrial units were established, mainly that of furniture making, aluminium and plastic goods manufacturing, tuna canning, repair shops and fertilizers. Further, nearly 9000 jobs were created in 36 industries in EPZ areas mainly in electronics, toys, garments as well in diamond cutting and polishing etc. (Mauritian Economic Review, 1976, Mehta, 1981).

In 1973, the increase of world sugar prices provided outstanding sugar yields, resulting in inflows of increased money supply. This facilitated joint ventures of sugar companies with foreign investors to enhance the EPZ and the tourist industry on the island. There was an overwhelming economic performance in this phase by effective policy implementation by the government through tax holiday, exemption from import duties and preferential access to European markets. In 1977, the number of EPZ rose to 88 and its export to 20 percent of total exports. The savings and investments were high and 32,000 jobs were created with the average annual real economic growth of 8.2 percent for the period 1971-77 displaying a peak of 16.6 percent in 1976.

However, the third phase of economic growth during 1978 to 1983 presented a dismal economic scenario of the country. The average real growth declined to 1.7 percent and the budget deficit situation worsened mainly due to heavy public expenditure incurred by the government, increase in import inflow and inadequate export outflow, resulting in a larger deficit in the balance of payments and a raised inflation rate of 42 percent in 1980. This situation of collapsing Mauritian economy was mainly caused by increased consumption and imports during the sugar boom followed by construction boom during euphoria years of economic prosperity, soaring oil prices due to world oil crises in 1977-80, and inflated airfares having adverse effects on the tourists' industry. Besides, the unemployment situation worsened and in 1982, there were as many as 73,000 jobless persons. In 1979, the government adopted the structural adjustment programme of the International Monetary Fund (IMF) by having fiscal stabilization; exchange rate realignment, cautious wage policies. There was a devaluation of Mauritian rupee by 30 percent in October 1979 (incidentally, Shiv R. Mehta, one of the authors was also a victim of this devaluation), followed by another devaluation (20 percent) to correct the over-valuation of the rupee, as that was impeding export development. In 1981, the inflation rate slipped to 14 percent and the economy started adjusting itself to take advantage of the devaluation of the rupee (Nath and Madhoo, 2003).

Only from 1983 onwards, the Mauritian economy got a shot in the arm. Employment situations improved considerably as the demand for labour due to expansion of export-oriented industries rose and by 1988, the numbers of unemployment were restricted to 16,000 only and the average real output growth was about 7 percent. The investment rate rose to 28.2 percent in 1988 while the saving rate went up to 28.6 percent in 1986. The balance of payment situation changed from a deficit of 15 percent of GDP to a surplus of 5 percent during 1983 to 1987. The inflation rate got dropped to 0.6 percent in 1987, making EPZ sector more competitive and their number rose to 591.

The wage structure was revised and the enhanced wages both in the public and private sectors led to a sharp increase in personal consumption besides reduction of a duty on a number of consumer goods and expansion in economic activities and employment situation. This was the period of Foreign Direct Investment (FDI)-Export-led rapid growth in Mauritius.

There was further diversification and consolidation of growth in Mauritius during 1989 to 2002. In two decades period (1983 to 2002). Mauritius economic transformation was witnessed as the economy moved from a mono-crop sugarcane dependence yielding sugar to the diversified one in having manufacturing and service sectors. In 1989, the offshore centre, was started which obtained more than $5 billion of offshore funds. Further, opening of stock exchange of Mauritius in the same period and creation of free port in 1992, helped in developing this nation as a regional trade centre. It is observed that in 1997, tourism increased by 10 percent, the EPZ by 6 percent, financial services by 5.9 percent and sugar by 5.5 percent and the inflation rate was 6.6 percent. In 1998, at the World Economic Forum, Mauritius was named the most competitive economy in Africa. It was ranked 29th in the World Competitiveness Report of 1999, as first among African countries and even outperforming some "Asian Tigers" (Nath and Madhoo, 2003).

It is observed that Mauritius is one of the few countries in Sub-Saharan Africa to have a steady real growth of around 5 percent per annum, on an average over the last three decades, with per capita GNP of about US$ 3,975 in the year 2000. Further, the share of manufacturing in GDP has risen from 6.5 percent in the early 1970s to around 23 percent in the late 1980s, while the agriculture share has declined from 34 percent in the early 1970s to 9.2 percent in the late 1990. This decline has been replaced partly by the service sector, which has stabilized its contribution to GDP at around 6.6 percent since the early 1980s. In 2000, the service sector contribution was 70 percent to GDP at factor cost, while manufacturing sector accounted for 24 percent and primary sector stood only at about 6 percent. Service sector has three main sub sectors such as whole sale and retail trade; restaurant and hotel, financing, insurance, real estate and business services, and transport, storage and communication. Besides, Mauritius is venturing to establish the cyber city to promote information and communication technology. It is argued that in view of Mauritius opening up to market economy by way of having imports and exports as the major share contributors in its national income, and dismantling of trade barriers, further increasing its exposure to the world market, there is a need for an appropriate regime to promote greater competitive culture not only in business to enhance efficiency in resource allocation and promote consumer welfare but also in Government and society in general, for an inclusive development (Mehta, P, 2006).

Mauritian economy did show a downward trend and grew at 4 percent in 2002, while in 2001, it was growing at 5.8 percent and had shown the annual average of 5.75 percent for the last two decades. Cyclone Dina in January 2002, hitting hard the sugar sector, the slow recovery of the US and European economies, the effects of 9/11 and political instability in Madagascar, have been identified as the main factors slowing down the island economy. The strength of Mauritian economy is based on three pillars, that is, sugar, export processing zones (EPZs) and tourism, but the

"Mauritian Miracle" is largely influenced by several factors such as Mauritian nationals owning about 50 percent of the total equity of EPZ firms, a restrictive trade regime by keeping exports relatively open but imports closed, segregating export sector from the import sector by having duty free access to all imported goods but keeping out the export sector in world markets, tax incentives to firms in the EPZ and by keeping labour market for the export sector effectively segmented from the rest of the economy (Employers in the EPZ had greater flexibility in discharging workers and paying incentives . Majority of women workers in EPZs were paid lower than their counterparts in the other sectors of economy. In 1980s their wages were 36-40 percent lower than that in the rest of economy).

In addition to above factors, as stated earlier, Mauritius, also enjoyed preferential access to USA and EU markets for sugar, textiles and clothing; its ethnic composition was instrumental to attract investment from the far East and its participatory coalition politics provided a stable political environment for its economic miracle which made it rise from a poorer country with per capita income of just $260 (in nominal terms) in early 1960s to a middle income country with a per capita income of about $3800 today (Subramanian and Ray 2002, Suchs and Warner, 1995, 1999 as quoted in Economic Report of Africa, 2003). However, it is observed that in short or medium terms, sugar, EPZs and tourism may grow but there is impending fear of losing preferential access to major industrial countries, affecting adversely the growth potential for sugar and EPZ products. Even tourism may reach its capacity in terms of geographic and environmental constraints. Faced by these realities, Mauritius is re-engineering itself to move up the value chain and build a knowledge led economy based on financial services, information and communication technologies, and modernization of sugar and EPZ sectors through higher productivity, better technology and greater capitalization (Mauritius Economic Report on Africa, 2003).

In 2005, Mauritius had a per capita GDP of \$ 12000 (PPP) and on that basis; it has been classified as a Middle Income Country. In fact, the income, since Independence, has risen 15-fold while, there has been decline of the same in other African nations. Tourism and export oriented textile production mainly developed and expanded by investors from Hong Kong, Taiwan, South Korea and Singapore, were the two main inputs in promoting economic development. The State political apparatus has skilfully deployed the preferential tariffs granted in respect of sugar under *Lome-Agreement* with the EU markets and to a lesser extent, the chances provided by the U.S. Agreement on *Growth and Opportunity Act (AGOA)* for clothing and textiles. Besides, Mauritius has exploited the high-end tourism to find 63rd ranking position on Human Development Index and even a higher ranking on Life Expectancy Index (73 years), the Education Index (0.8) and the Human Poverty Index (only 11 percent of the population are classified as poor, that is, living on less than a \$ a day). Despite that, there are glaring inequalities observed particularly between the Franco-Mauritian upper class and the people of other ethnic groups, especially the Creoles. In economic terms, Mauritius is encountering crises in its various sectors, especially in textile and sugar. No doubt, a growth rate of 3.4 percent was observed in 2005 –06 due to a boom in the tourist industry, yet the unemployment rate which was around 5.6 percent in 1990s, went up to around 10 percent in 2005-06, mainly because of growing number of unemployed in the Export Processing Zones (Bertelsmann Stifung, BTI, Mauritius Country Report, 2008).

Critical Appraisal of Mauritius's Economic "Miracle"

In the immediate post independent era, sugar boom helped not only the millers and sugar estate magnets to appropriate maximum profits but also the small planters mostly belonging to the Hindu ethnic stock because of assured price of sugar in the world market under *Lome* convention. This had two main effects. There was a construction boom on the island and people started constructing pucca houses after replacing tin and asbestos sheds in the villages and towns. Besides, people especially the Indo-Mauritians not only improved their life styles but encouraged their children to go in for higher education to India, U.K. and France. After completion of education abroad, many of them were absorbed in the new bureaucratic structure created by the political system, preponderantly occupied by the people of Indian origin. The capitalist path of development was visible. The nation was on the move as a consumerist society because people were largely attracted to modern gadgets like TV sets, Hi-Fi music systems, luxury cars, refrigerators, cooking range, rice cookers and other household appliances. "Buy now and pay later" schemes and other loan facilities through financial institutions and banks, made the people move towards a credit oriented society. Because of the widening income disparities in between different ethnic groups, the inequalities further got enhanced. No doubt, a new middle class characterized by "white collar" syndrome was emerging but this class was fascinated by luxuries, gadgets and comfort providing devices which became needs rather than demands. There was malnourishment observed among the poorer section of people especially the Creoles and the Muslims. As such, during 1970s, the most beneficiary of the developmental inputs were Franco-Mauritians followed by Sino-Mauritians (Chinese), Indo-Mauritians (Both Hindus and Muslims) and Afro-Mauritians (African Creoles) in that order. Poverty ratios were higher in rural than urban areas and more so among African Creoles. (The dock workers (labourers) and other workers in sugar estates, were observed to be interested in possessing modern gadgets than investing in nourishing their children and lactating mothers etc., even after availing of the end of the year salary bonus). There used to be one big shopping complex (Prisunic) owned and managed by the French multinational. But other multinationals were also active in dealing with electronics, garments, beach hotels and resorts, shipping, airways, import of food items etc. Their caucus was strong and through their dubious ways and means (double pricing system, air ticketing and hotel bookings done at the place of embarkment etc.) left hardly any option for the state to generate revenue because of the flight of money either to another country or the cities having their corporate offices.

Notwithstanding the above developments, till 1980, the economy of the island started showing strains and there was slow down of the same from 1983 to 1988 due to factors already identified. But there was a spurt of infrastructure and technological developments such as highways, expressways, irrigation and power generation, means of transportation, telecommunication, mobile phones, computers, cyber city centres providing BPO services, digital cameras, big shopping complexes and Malls (Jumbo, Shoprite and Winnie etc.), multi-storey buildings, commercial flats, five-star hotels, beach resorts and flats, luxury cars of all brands from Germany, France, U.S.A., Britain and Japan, entry of multinationals in durable and non-durable consumer goods and services. Apart from these changes, the institutional changes pertaining to banking, financial institutions related to off shore banking, import and export, sugar syndicate for small planters, sugar labour welfare fund, educational and medical care institutions (hospital, medical colleges and dispensaries), higher education through the strengthening of University Faculties etc have not only brought a change in the life style and consumption pattern of the people but there appears a change in the outlook of the people as well. Most of them have developed more rational orientation and they tend to be more personalized and self oriented in their behaviour pattern than before. Time is becoming scarce and instead of institutions serving the people, they have become captive of them. Better social service oriented changes like education, health care services and population control measures, may have also contributed significantly in improving the quality of life of people at large. Even the liberal democracy practiced on the Island through participation of people from the different segments of population in electing their representatives, may have made them conscious of their rights for a good society, characterized by tension and disruption free life.

But, the moot question is whether Mauritius has acquired a societal formation or not? There is no doubt, that one may observe a movement of the island community towards the emergence of society, which is still ridden with tensions or disruptions. These may be latent and not manifest themselves, not only in economic but also in social relationships. These may be simmering underneath the surface and may disturb the harmony of people, if not handled adequately by the state machinery. We do know that tensions cause social change but it is also true that the social change causes tensions in a society. For the kind of social and economic changes observed on the island, we need to examine the income distribution pattern, expenditure pattern, employment status, and incidence of poverty as indicators of economic development. Further, we need to evaluate the role of four pillars such as sugar, EPZ, tourism and information technology sectors upon which the future of this nation rests and suggest the ways ahead for its development.

It is reported that the average monthly household income increased by 33.7 percent from Rs. 14,232 in 2001-02 to Rs. 19,025 in 2006-2007. However, after adjusting for inflation during the above period, there was hardly any change in the household income. Further, the income inequality had increased in the above period as the share of total income enjoyed by 20 percent of household, at the lower end of income range decreased from 6.4 percent in 2001-02 to 6.1 percent in 2006-07 while that of upper 20 percent of households increased from 44 percent to 45.7 percent (An increase in Gini Coefficient from 0.371 in 2001-02 to 0.389 in 2006-07 confirms a rise in income inequality brought at par with that in 1996-97 (0.387)). Besides, there is no change observed in the average number of earners per household after adjusting for household size (1.8 earners for an average household size of 3.7 in 2006-07 as compared to 1.9 in 2001-02 for a household size of 3.9) Wage and salaries constituted the main source of household income (69.4 percent of total gross income in 2006-07 against 69.8 percent in 2001-02), besides transfer income mainly of pensioners and other social security benefits (13.2 percent of total gross income in 2006-07 against 10.6 percent in 2001-02).

Against increased income, the average monthly household consumption expenditure also shot up by 33.3 percent from Rs. 11,390 in 2001-02 to Rs 15,188 in 2006-07. However, after adjusting for inflation and the decrease in household size for the above period, the real increase of the consumption expenditure of private households is nearly 5 percent. This household expenditure was highest for food and "non-alcoholic beverages" (30 percent) followed by transport (15.2 percent), housing, water, electricity, gas and other fuels (9.8 percent) and alcoholic beverages and tobacco (9.5 percent). Besides, "education" saw the highest increase in the household expenditure (87 percent) followed by 'communication' (58 percent) and 'alcoholic beverages and tobacco (48 percent) while in 'miscellaneous goods and services' it was only 30 percent.

As regards the incidence of relative poverty, worked on the basis of the half median monthly household income per adult equivalent, it was 8.0 percent in 2006-07, up from 7.7 percent in 2001-02, as the number of poor households increased from 23,700 in 2001-02 to 26,900 in 2006-07. (Economic and Social Indicators, Central Statistics Office, Mauritius, 2007). The poverty ratio has been observed more in rural (9.1 percent) than urban (6.9 percent) and semi urban (6.3 percent) areas, besides a higher proportion of female headed (widowed, divorced/separated) households, than males, were in the poverty group. (Central Statistics Office, Poverty Analysis, Mauritius, 2001-02).

A cursory look at the above statistics closely indicates that without any change in real income over a period of six years or so, the expenditure pattern of people in the island has risen considerably. This is indicative of the Mauritian people tending to be consumer oriented and in order to meet their consumer demands, which have now become their needs, they have no option but to seek credits from different institutional and non-institutional sources. Income disparities are also widening, as the upper 20 percent of the households seem to be enjoying the fruits of development much more than those in the lower 20 percent category. Over-consumption and increasing inequalities are not the true indicators of development despite a rise in GDP, maintained at 5 percent per annum over a period of three decades. This rise in GDP is not to be taken as a growth signal as it masks many social and economic realities because as sociologists, we are interested in conditions in which people live.

It is observed that in view of non-availability of information on distribution of land and wealth in Mauritius, the differentials in income distribution and wages become the only indicator for analysing the improvement in income distribution. Employment situation rose by 150 percent between 1983 and 1989 before stabilizing during 1990s. Real wages were initially flat but showed upward trends in mid 1980s and continued through the 1990s, after that these had stopped rising. The labour productivity fell by 20 percent during the period of rapid labour absorption but it got stabilized and rose gradually during the 1990s. The low real wages during rapid employment expansion period were suggestive of a high elastic overall supply of labour in Mauritius as the wages and employment were expected to rise in export-oriented sectors but likely to fall in import-oriented sectors due to shifting structure of output. But, actually the results partially supported the above expectations. No doubt, employment in export sectors rose in response to trade liberalization but the real wage growth on the contrary fell in these sectors and employment and real wages in fact, expanded in the import sector. One reason could be that labour supply into manufacturing was not fixed and a very large supply in labour force helped females who were earlier unemployed or out of labour market to find employment in EPZ. Thus the elastic supply of female labour kept real wages low in EPZ while still maintaining employment in the import sector. Employment in agriculture was also observed to fall during this period, providing more impetus to employment in the manufacturing sector; the share of EPZ investment in it having risen from 12 percent in 1982 to 45 percent in 1985 (Nath and Madhoo, 2008).

The latest statistics indicate that out of a total of 565.9 (thousands) labour force in Mauritius in 2006, 515.8 (thousands) are in large establishments while 220.7 (thousands) are outside large establishments showing an overall unemployment status of 9.1 percent. The sex wise breakdown of unemployment rate is 5.5 percent for males and 15.5 percent for females. The minimum wage prescribed by the National Remuneration Board for a farm labourer in sugar cane is Rs. 5071 for male and for female, it is Rs. 3857 per month, while in the tea (Rs. 4746 for male and Rs. 3722 for female) and Tobacco, (Rs. 4746 for male and Rs. 3722 for female, it is lower). These are still lower in the export enterprises (It is Rs. 2526). However, in sugarcane plantations, a worker gets about Rs. 11,854 per month while in textile, a factory worker gets Rs. 7,400 per month, the range of monthly earning varies from Rs. 23,684 (Reporter and Journalist and Bank Clerk Rs. 23,455) to a scavenger/ street sweeper drawing Rs. 3,118 per month. It is apparent from these statistics, that monthly earning for an employee in typical occupations in selected industries (excluding government) is in the ratio of 7:1, thus showing a varied salary structure. The highest paid in the government sector is a Medical and Health Officer (Rs. 36,468/- per month) and the lowest paid is a labourer (Rs. 8,448 per month) (Central Statistics Office, Annual Digest of Statistics, 2006).

No doubt, the GDP rate is on the rise (around 6-7 percent) but the inflation rate is also on the higher side, say it is hovering around 8 percent per annum. This may hit badly the common man and especially those in the salary brackets. As such, there is a dire need to revise the wage and salary structure of employees in private and public sector establishments. A step in this direction is already on the move in this fiscal year (2008-09). Further, there is a need to tackle the unemployment status both for males and females (Females are worst affected because of slowing down of EPZs and shutting down of some of them) to take care of the incidence of poverty especially in the rural areas.

Economic Transformation: Futuristic Trends

What is the economic future of Mauritius? Is it still agriculture, dominated by a mono-crop of sugarcane or Is it

Export Processing Zone manufacturing industries or is it tourism that has and is developing Mauritius infrastructally to the international standards or does it rest on the new "mantra" of information and communication technology which is both fascinating and challenging for growth and development of the country? We shall, make an attempt to analyse the contribution of each of these in the context of development of this island nation.

No doubt, of the total land area of 186500 hectares on the island, agriculture accounts for 46.2 percent (86,500 hectares) yet sugarcane utilization of land was only 76,840 hectares (41.2 percent) in the year 1995. In 2006, it has come down to 70,810 hectares while the other crops like Tea and Tobacco utilize 688 hectares and 252 hectares of land area respectively. Sugar cane production is reported to be 4,749,000 tons in 2006 while that of tea (green leaf processed) is 7649 tons and tobacco leaf is only 298 tons, vegetable pulses and fruits production for 2006 is 103,881 tons (the highest that of creepers followed by mixed vegetables and tomatoes and bananas in that order). The fish catch in 2006 is reported to be 8,623 (wet weight metric tons, including coastal fishing and High sea (6,333 metric tons). Besides, of the total cattle heads 10,999, local breeds including bulls and calves and cows, account only 221 whereas the imported breed number is 10,421.

Interestingly , the area under sugarcane cultivation in the case of Millers has come down from 38.8 thousand hectares in 2000 to 30.5 thousand hectares in 2006. But in the case of planters, for the same period, it has risen from 38.2 thousand hectares to 40.3 thousand hectares. The area harvested and the cane harvested show similar trends, lower for millers and higher for the planters. However, the average yield (tons per hectare) is higher in respect of millers (79.4) than planters(65.4) in 2006 and the sugar price (exsyndicate) for the same year is reported to be Rs. 17,350 per ton, an increase over the price of 2000, which was Rs.11,570 per/ton. However, the number of factories now in operation for manufacturing of white sugar, raw sugar, molasses and scums have come down from 14 in 2000 to 10 in 2006. Sugar production (504,857 tons) and molasses production (139,621 tons) have also declined over the years from 2001 to 2006. (Central Statistics Office, Annual Digest of Statistics, 2006, July 2007).

The above statistics clearly bring out that sugar mills are on the decline and the stakeholders for the same are diversifying either to other manufacturing units like making ethanol products from molasses or they are entering into tourism industry and investing in beach hotels, resorts, restaurants and real estate business. They have been joined in these enterprises by the affluent Chinese both belonging to local population and those immigrated from Far East regions (Hong Kong, Singapore, Taiwan etc.) The Franco-Mauritian and Sino-Mauritian, by and large, have adherence to the Christian faith and in that sense, they have better business understanding and accommodation between them.

In the light of the above observations, it is difficult to visualize the future of Mauritius in the field of agriculture especially sugarcane as a major crop for the development of the economy.

Even Export Processing Zones (EPZs) are shrinking, manufacture of wearing apparel units have come down from 313 in 2003 to 292 in 2004. Even the energy requirement (total primary energy requirement (1990=100)) is not encouraging and is rising from 158.4 in 2002 to 188.1 in 2006 and its import dependency in 2006 is 81.5 percent. Even, both the sugar and EPZ sectors, no longer enjoy the preferential treatment of EU markets and USA, despite their modernization. However, the modernization programmes in these are making them more capital intensive, demanding less labour and higher skills. That may cause unemployment especially among the unskilled labour, which is already hovering around 9 percent. Many of them will slide down to the poverty group. This may tantamount to mal-development or anti-developmental strategy. The danger is, that the capital-intensive technology may result in the jobless growth in the economy. As such, there is a need to look for labour-intensive activities that may generate employment and reduce poverty dimension on the island.

Another significant pillar of economic "miracle" is tourism. No doubt, over the years, tourist arrivals have been on increase in Mauritius (57,085 tourists in the year 1999 while in 2006, their number stood at 788,276). The majority of them are drawn in from France, United Kingdom, Reunion island, South Africa (Republic), Italy, Germany and India in that order. Even the tourists' nights have gone up from 5729,464 to 7,769,679 during the period 1999 to 2006 while the bed occupancy rate has risen from 59 in 2005 to 62 in 2006 (Central Statistics Office, Annual Digest of Statistics, 2006-07).

Employment generation has been created by tourism industry through hotels and restaurants as in 2004, it stood at 18,476 while in 2006, it was 21,341. Sex wise breakdown suggests that it was more for males than females (Male: 14505 in 2004 and 16,298 in 2006 and Female: 3971 in 2004 and 5043 in 2006) but it has not been substantial and because of dubious ways and means adopted by MNCs which own hotels and tourist resorts (air ticketing and room booking paid in the countries of tourists' origin than in Mauritius), the state does not earn much of revenue unlike in sugar industry where a toll tax has been imposed on the sale of sugar proceeds. Besides, there is a need for professional managerial skills to manage the hotels and resorts efficiently to provide world class services. Mauritius has to have professional management Institutes in these fields to attract diverse number of tourists. Cyclone fury, rise in crime rates especially theft, robbery, dacoity, rape, murder etc, and other social evils associated with tourism such as child abuse, prostitution and environmental hazards need to be tackled by state apparatus to make tourism as an attractive economic proposition.

The hope of the state, perhaps, now rests on the new pillar of economic miracle that is, information and communication technology as a knowledge based developmental input because tourism may soon reach its capacity of geographic and environmental constraints. Besides, the sector of information technology, another important knowledge based sector, is expanding financial sector. Both these sectors require skilled labour force. However, the educational composition of labour face shows that the nation is not equipped to meet the requirements of knowledge based economy. It is observed that unemployment is mostly prevailing among young people (24 years old or younger) who do not complete primary education and are in fact unemployed and do not complete secondary education (World Bank 2002). As such, creating new jobs in the knowledge economy may not help most of the unqualified (Mauritius, Economic Report of Africa, 2003).

A cyber city (Ebene) is being developed to promote information technology industry by Indians and Chinese to take advantage of the Mauritian bilingual workforce and the telecommunications to provide launching pad for Africa and beyond. The state is evolving a strategy that attracts highly skilled labour force by investing in education, reforming labour laws to attract foreign professionals, investing in physical infrastructure and providing incentives similar to EPZs to attract local and international investments.

But the real bottleneck is the increasing unemployment especially among females by the closure of textile mills and capital-intensive investment enterprises.

It is observed that unemployment is partly structural because of a big mismatch in job requirements and job aspirations. In spite of high unemployment, there are nearly 17,000 foreign guest workers mainly employed in the EPZs, in comparison to the unemployed labour force of 18,000 in 2001 (IMF 2002b). Mauritians think jobs in EPZs are less secure and lowly paid than those elsewhere (nearly 33 percent of females in the labour force as compared to 66 percent of males above 15 years of age are in employment and the majority of them are enjoying lower wages than men in EPZs). Even, those employed in the EPZs are considered by their employers to have low productivity than foreign workers. As a consequence of these factors, nearly 30 percent of the workers in textile and clothing manufacturing are brought from outside the country. A rise in wages is another serious matter to be taken in account that contributes to higher unemployment (In 2001, the average compensation per worker increased by 7.1 percent and the labour productivity by 5.0 percent, indicating that the unit labour costs in dollars is declining and the country depends on currency depreciation to stay competitive). As such, there is a diversification of production based on higher value-added activities such as those in financial and information technology sectors. But these sectors demand a highly skilled labour, at least trained graduates and diploma holders. Mauritian labour market may find it difficult to supply the highly skilled manpower to manage the knowledge based economy as an average Mauritian worker has completed 7 years of education, compared with 10 years in Singapore and 9 in China and the Republic of Korea (World Bank 2002). Besides, nearly 1/3rd of students, mostly from poor families fail to complete primary education and drop out at 12 to 13 year age, with not enough good vocational schools to upgrade their skills for a new economy. (Mauritius, Economic Reform of Africa, 2003).

The Way Ahead

In view of the above, what is the way ahead for the Mauritian economy?

Sugar which accounted for 50 percent of agricultural growth on the island to the tune of about 8 percent of GDP, enjoyed preferential access to European markets for nearly half a century through the sugar protocol and Social Preferential Sugar Agreement (Mauritius received guaranteed price at some 100-200percent above World Market Prices and guaranteed market share through quotas and the cumulative benefit to the tune of $3.5 billion between 1975 and 2000) (IMF 2002A). This preferential quota for Mauritius has already been reduced drastically and it was to be eliminated by 2007. With the price of sugar falling in the world market because of cheap availability of beet than cane sugar, its sugar production is threatened and the sugar industry has initiated its reforms to ensure that 3500 workers should opt for voluntary retirement scheme and nearly three sugar factories should close down and offer training programmes to the retired workers. All the above requirements were duly met by the sugar industry by December 31, 2007 (5600 persons opted for VRS scheme, three sugar factories namely St. Felix, Mont Tresur Mon Desert and Riche en Eau have stopped milling after the harvest of 2007 and 1500 former employees have been enrolled for training. Two more factories Desert Almen and Mou Loisir are planning to close in 2008). In 2008, the sugar industry is to shift to be a cane industry thereby, affecting the production of refined sugar and other by-products such as ethanol and electricity by 2009. It is expected that by 2009-10, the sugar factories number will be reduced to four with the number of employees brought down to 750 only (Curpen, Indra Dev, News on Sunday, Jan 11-17, 2008). So sugar industry as a contributor to Mauritian economy, has practically no future.

Even the manufacturing sector grew at a slower rate of 2.20 percent in 2002, mainly because there was a slowdown in Export Processing Zones and other manufacturing activities such as food processing, beverages, cosmetics, fertilizers, footwear, furniture, paint and sugar milling etc. Prospects for garment manufacturing were also weakening as preferential access to major markets was getting eroded due to phasing out of Multifibre Agreement by the end of 2004, giving tough competition to Mauritus from other competitors in Far East. Tourism, which was also providing 6 percent contribution to national GDP, fell sharply in its growth from 13.6 percent in 2000 to 1 percent in 2001, in terms of tourist arrivals, mainly because of world recession and cancellation of travel projects after 9/11 attacks in U.S.A. However, it picked up later on, as expenditure per tourist, room occupancy rates and employment situation improved during the last few years despite a rise in average nominal expenditure per tourist (in rupees). In fact, it has been made a high-end tourist destination by providing international level facilities. But, the fear expressed is, that Mauritius may soon lose its geographic environmental and social limits to expand tourism because as indicated by a study done in 1998, there has to be a cultural impact limit of 750, 000 tourists and an environmental limit not beyond current arrivals of 680,000. The state is emphasising on low-impact, high spending tourism and not to depend on one originating market (Europe) and one product (beach resort tourism) (Mauritius, Economic Report on Africa, 2003).

In the above backdrop, there is not much that the traditional pillars of economic miracle (sugar, EPZs, and tourism) have further potential to boost growth on the island. Even high-end knowledge based economy propelled by financial and information technology institutional development has its limitation as without highly skilled manpower, their growth potential will not be fully realized. Even if the expatriates from different parts of the world having expertise, are to be hired, these sectors shall not be cost effective as the expenditure incurred on them shall become unbearable for the State apparatus and instead of generating economic growth, these may boomerang and affect the development process adversely.

In view of the latest world food crisis and fuelling of price rise of consumable food commodities due to spiral rise of petrol cost (touching as high as $ 140 per barrel but this has come down recently), Mauritius political structure must look inwards instead of over relying on export oriented products and revive its traditional agricultural sector. Instead of cutting down on sugar cane cultivation, the sugar magnets and barons, need to be convinced by the polity that they should take up the market vegetable gardens. There has been a traditional habit of residents especially in rural areas of having kitchen-garden in the front or backyards of their houses and the skills developed in these efforts could be fruitfully utilized for producing vegetables on a large scale to meet the growing needs of the consumers. Besides, the government in cooperation with the private owners of sugar estates should enter into public-private partnership, to identify land areas for rice cultivation, as rice is a stable diet for most of the Mauritians. Similarly, increased areas should be brought under pulses cultivation of different varieties so that the cost involved in their imports is brought to the minimum desirable level. Allied agricultural products like milk, fishery and poultry should be encouraged to utilise the traditional skills of people in rural areas for meeting the requirements of the growing population. These ventures can be pursued on a large scale by combining labour-intensive and capital-intensive activities. There used to be around 25,000 cows on the island at the time a study was done by one of the authors (Shiv. R. Mehta, 1981) but now fresh milk was observed to be a rare commodity.

To make these realize fully, the government must review their thinking and adopt sound rural development policies and programmes for effective implementation of these to tackle the growing problem of unemployment and poverty on the island. It may be argued in certain quarters that due to widespread of education, youth below 24 years who are mostly unemployed may not like to dirty their hands in agricultural or other allied activities like milching cattle or poultry rearing or fishing but there are school dropouts, who can be trained in vocational centres to develop skills around these activities. It was also mentioned by one of our key informants that in view of most of the females having joined EPZs, they are not interested in labour intensive activities of the above nature. But, the counter argument is that by engaging themselves with such activities, they shall remain close to their families and look after their children as well. Besides, they shall save on transport charges incurred by them to move from one place to another and the lower wages paid to them, shall get neutralized in that way.

The roots of Indo-Mauritians who are mostly settled in rural areas are group centered (family-kinship complex) and their shift to individual oriented personalized behaviour pattern, has led to status inconsistency, ambivalent attitude and acquisition of non-moralistic values, making Mauritius a dissatisfied consumer oriented and an emerging "at risk" society. Moral must go along with material to develop a balanced society as the materialistic outlook of an individual tends to make him or her mercenary rather then altruistic, educated but not learnt, selfish rather selfless or as one showing concern or mutual help and love for others. Mauritius may have passed beyond the threshold point of a communitarian life and entered into a societal formation but if it undervalues the moral dimensions of development, it shall land itself into the same crises as is being witnessed in developed nations of Western Europe and U.S.A. Development must be conceived in cultural specific sense and since the majority of population (Indo-Mauritian, say about 3/4th of total population) belong to cultural groups that value morals than materials, the development strategy should be in consonance with that, otherwise it will prove anti-developmental.

References

Bertelsmann Stiftung, BTI 2008; (2007), *Mauritius Country Report*, Gutersloh.

Carpen Indradev (2008), Sugar Poised for Reform", *News on Sunday*, Jan 11-17, Mauritius.

Central Statistics Office, Republic of Mauritius (2001-02), *Poverty Analysis*.

Central Statistics Office, Republic of Mauritius (2007). *Economic and Social Indicators*, Issue Number 664.

Central Statistics Office, Republic of Mauritius (2006-07), *Annual Digest of Statistics*.

Economic Report on Africa (2003) " Chapter 8, *Mauritius-Moving up the Value Chain*" pp. 247-281.

Gallop, J. Sachs, J. and Mellinger A, (1999) "Geography and Economic Development", *NBER Working Papers 6849*, National Bureau of Economic Research, Inc.

International Monetary Fund (IMF) (2001), "*Mauritius 2001: Staff Report*" Washington D.C.

International Monetary Fund (IMF) (2002a), "*Mauritius 2002: Staff Report*" Washington D.C.

International Monetary Fund (IMF) (2002b), "*Mauritius Selected issues and Statistical Appendix*", Washington D.C.

Jeffery, Alexander (1990), "*Democracy and Civil Society, Watergate and the Discourse of Civil Society*", Department of Sociology, Los Angeles, University of California (Draft Chapter).

Lal, Brij, (Marvin in) (2007) (Ed.) "Mauritius" *The Encyclopaedia of the Indian Diaspora*, Singapore, University of Singapore, pp. 263-272.

Limao, N and Venables A. (2001) "Infrastructure geographical disadvantage, Transport Costs and Trade", *The World Bank Economic Review*, Vol. 15 (3) pp. 451-479.

Meade, J et. al (1961). *The Economic and Social Structure of Mauritius*, Meuthen, London.

Mauritius, 1976, *Mauritius Economic Review*, Ministry of Economic Planning and Development.

Mehta, S.R., (1981), *Social Development in Mauritius: A Study on Rural Modernization in an Island Community*, New Delhi, Wiley Eastern Ltd.

Mehta, S.R. (1989) " The Uneven Inclusion of Indian Immigrants in Mauritius" *Sociological Bulletin*, 38 (1), March, reproduced in Jayaram N (Ed.) (2004) *The Indian Diaspora: Dynamics of Migration*, New Delhi, Sage Publications, pp 186-199.

Mehta, S.R. (1999), *Dynamics of Development: A Sociological Perspective*, New Delhi, Gyan Publishing House.

Nath Shyam and Madhoo Yeti Nisha (2003) "Explaining African Economic Growth Performance: The Case of Mauritius, *African Economic Research Consortium*, Nairobi, Kenya (Typescript) pp 1-45.

Nath Shyam and Madhoo Yeti Nisha (2008) "A shared growth story of economic success: The case of Mauritius" Chapter 11 in *The*

Political Economy of Economic Growth of Africa, 1960-2000 (Eds) Ndulu, Benno J. et. al, Cambridge, Cambridge University Press pp1-58.

Perru, Reshma, et. al (2006) "*Mauritius in Competition Regimes in the World- A Civil Society Report*" (Ed.). Mehta, S. Pradeep, CUTS International and International Network of Civil Society Organisation in Competitions (INCSOC) Jaipur, pp. 246-251.

Rodrik, D. (1999) *The New Global Economy and Developing Countries: Making Openness Work*, London, Overseas Development Council.

Roomer, P (1992) "The strategies for Economic Development. Using Ideas and Producing Ideas", *Proceedings of the Annual Conference on Development Economics*, Washington, D.C.

Sachs, J Warner, A (1997) "Sources of Slow Growth in African Economies" *Journal of African Economics,* Vol. 6, pp. 35-376.

Subramaniam A and Roy, D. (2001) *Who can explain the Mauritian Miracle: Meade, Romer, Sachs or Rodrick,* International Monetary Fund, African Department, Washington D.C.

Weaver, James H (1975), "Economic Development: Two Paradigms" *Development Studies Programme*, Agency for International Development, Washington D.C. (Transcript of a Talk).

World Bank (2002) "Mauritius Country Assistance Strategy" *Report 23904 HAS African Region*, Country Department, 8 Washington, D.C.

4

Power Struggle of Coalition Politics

Power Dynamics in Politics

Anthropologists have studied many achephalous or stateless societies where the two dimensions of power, that is, control and influence operate through kinship-family network influence. However, modern societies as nation-states have evolved mechanisms or apparatuses through governmentalization processes or influences to manage the affairs of people inhabiting a territory or an area, in a regulated manner through laws or rules that take care of their voices, protests and dissents, to provide social justice to them in an equitable manner. As such, politics which analyses the distribution of power within the state, provides privileged position to power holders who head the helm of affairs and assume responsibility for the production, distribution and consumption of resources in a planned manner for the good of a society.

It is observed that most of the conflicts in a society are mainly due to efforts on the part of individuals or groups to either capture or share power to have a hold on decision-making processes to take an advantageous position against others who are competing with them with a different set of ideas and values.

In the light of the above, we need to understand the concepts of power and politics. Power, in the Weberian sense, implies allowing or not allowing individuals or groups to achieve certain ends or goals or acquire possessions of things or objects that they desire, wish or aspire most. Power in a totalitarian or autocratic system, can be accomplished or achieved through the use of coercion or force by employing dictatorial means. In this system, the communication between the leaders and the led is one way and often vertical from top-downwards. Power, in this sense, may be viewed as an absolute one and may assume an extreme form when demonstrated in master-slave relationship in which obedience of orders by the slaves is sacrosanct and any violation of that has to be met with punishment of physical torture, resulting in severe injuries to the inflicted persons. This is nothing short of display of 'naked' power. However, in modern societies, nation-states have evolved political systems that provide governance to its people or subjects by not resorting to coercion or force but through persuasions, appeals, justifications to influence them to take part in the decision making processes, for the establishment of a good society. This is what the societies opting for democratic governance through a consensus building mechanisms are trying to experiment, with a varying degree of success. More and more nation-states in the world are joining the bandwagon of democratic governance. During the last two decades or so, nearly 40 of them have gone in for this option.

The concepts of politics and political system need to be understood to analyse the power dynamics of a nation-state. No doubt, the concept of society preceded to that of state but the state formation evolved an efficient and effective apparatus to pursue and achieve the well-defined goals for the welfare of its people, that is its citizens. It is argued that all states whether traditional or modern, have a political apparatus or system (governmental institutions such as a court, parliament or congress, plus civil-services officials), which rules over a given territory and whose authority is backed by a legal system having sanctions to enforce and implement its policies. Even in Weberian sense, power when legitimised becomes authority. Power, no doubt is an all pervasive aspect of human relationships and is based on the ability of individuals or members of a group to accomplish or achieve aims or further the interest they hold, whereas politics denote the means by which power is used to influence the nature and context of governmental activities. "Political", as such, not only includes activities of those in government but also of many other groups and individuals whose actions in many ways, outside the governmental set-up, influence it (Giddens, 1989).

Power holding or sharing in that sense becomes a phenomenon which involves political parties having conviction and different ideologies to struggle for commanding or influencing the decision-making processes affecting citizens within the state or nation-state for their survival, material and other welfare needs. It becomes, therefore, imperative to analyse the power structure of a group, community or society because it is only through that, the development goals would be pursued to bring in social and economic transformation of the people.

There are two landmark studies, which have provided different perspectives on the community power structure. Hunter's study (1963) on *Community Power Structure*, provides a monolithic pyramidal power structure where the leadership pattern depicts a triangular representation, the apex of the triangle represents the top leadership structure while the other leaders are down the apex to control or influence the mass base of people. The other contrasting leadership structure is analysed by Dahl (1961). The paradigm depicted represents a hexagon (two intersecting equilateral triangles above and below), showing a pluralized pattern where leadership is chosen through wider participation processes of people in the middle, to the shrinking of the mass base. These two paradigms of community power structures have been observed to be co-existing in societies, which are in transitional movement from traditional to modern social and economic arrangements. However, leadership is considered as an activity of controlling or influencing the behaviour of others towards the achievement of the determined goal while the community power structure is determined the way the leadership gets distributed in the group, community or society. The factors that give rise to leadership structure in the community or society are based on an individual's traits like, age, sex or personal qualities like education, wealth or income, the numerical or economic dominance of a particular group or economic dominance of individuals within a particular group and the situations in which the individuals and the groups are placed in the community in terms of their distribution on the basis of above characteristics. (Mehta, 1972).

In the above backdrop, we need to examine the factors in this tiny island nation, which has embraced parliamentary system of democratic governance after its independence in 1968. However, before that we have to look into the historical circumstances that gave rise to the freedom struggle for attainment of nationhood and subsequently to it the status of a sovereign republic.

The Political Rise of People of Indian Origin (Indo-Mauritians in the Pre-independent Period)

No doubt, the first generation of Indian immigrants struggled hard to find a place for themselves in positions of authority on the sugarcane plantations. This could become a possibility only as a result of the *morcellement* policy in the late 19th century that provided an opportunity to them to acquire land and become wealthy in the villages around sugar estates, yet they aspired that their children should become educated and acquire political elitism on the island. In fact, they were the harbingers of Indian religious and cultural values and maintained their identity as a group or groups (Both of the Hindu and Muslim ethnic stocks) to assert for their right to independence against the colonists (French and British). who held economic dominance.

However, it was Annasamy from the merchant class of Indo-Mauritians who was appointed to political office as a member of the unofficial colonial committee in 1827. Later on, from mid 19th century onwards, prominent members of the Tamil community such as Sinnatambour, Chetiar and Moonisamy were appointed to District Committees. Even some of the other wealthy families (Pitchen, Pragassa, Rayapa and Sandapa) by 1850, qualified to be on the electoral list. In 1880s, Governor Pope Hennessy, nominated Gyanadicrayen Arlanda and a number of Muslims to the Council of Government. A 'Calcuttya' Muslim (this term is employed for the indentured labourers of Muslim descendents not necessarily from North India but including Bhojpuri speaking Biharis), Abdoula Goolam Dustagheer, was the first, among 400 Indo-Mauritians qualified for the franchise, to stand for the elections in 1896 and 1901, but could not get elected despite getting some votes from outside his own community. However, Dr. Hassen Sakir of Lascar Muslim community was elected successfully as a Municipal Councillor in Port Louis in 1900 (Marin in Lal, 2007).

It was only in 1901 onwards that the political organization of Indo-Mauritians got on its way after a brief visit of Mahatma Gandhi who sent his envoy Manilal Doctor to the island in 1907 for the same. Not only Manilal Doctor started the Hindustani newspaper but also defended many cases of Indians in the court till his departure in 1911. The inducements of above nature motivated a number of other Hindu intellectuals, having risen from the ranks of indentured labourers, to make the colonists hear their voices of dissent or protest. Ramkelawon Boodhun, a barrister educated in Britain was son of an immigrant railway worker, who fought the general elections in 1921 and despite losing the seat, was nominated along with Dr. Hassen Sakir by the Governor, to represent Indo-Mauritians between 1921 and 1926. Another son of a Hindu immigrant Boodhun Lallah, was also actively involved in politics despite his losing to a white candidate in 1911 general elections. This was followed by a campaign launched against the *Retrocessionist Movement* wanting to seek reattachment with France by the Indo-Mauritians but this got fizzled out by caste differences. In 1926 general election, Rajcoomar Gujadhar of Bihar origin and Lalla, were elected under the banner of *l'Union Mauricienne*. At the same time, clerics from India and local "pandits" belonging to the Muslims and Hindu Communities, gave impetus to political mobilization (Marin in Lal, 2007).

Political Movement for Freedom of the Island

In continuation of the above process of political mobilization, there was a dramatic turn of events due to economic depression experienced during 1930s, and that radicalised the working class resulting into the formation of trade unions. It was Dr. Maurice Curie who founded the labour Party in 1936. However, the celebrations associated with the arrival of the indentured labourers from India on the completion of their century in 1935, had already acted as a catalyst to provide political mobilization. During 1940s, the Hindus were mobilized by Basdeo Bisoondoyal to raise their number as voters within the preview of a new Constitution in 1947 as that provided franchise to men and women having passed a literacy test. The number of electorates rose from fewer than 10,000 to more than 70,000. The election to the Legislative council was held in 1948 and it showed the real mobilization of the Indo-Mauritians. The Hindus captured a number of seats in districts where they had the majority while the Muslim candidates were wiped out completely, clearly depicting their minority status (Marin in Lal, 2007).

The first general election for the Party Elective Council for the entire island was held in 1886, which can hardly be called democratic, as out of total population of 3.65 million, only less than 12,000 were eligible to vote. However, hence onwards, these elections were held fairly on regular basis after every five years. But, the real political changes were observed only in 1948 after the Second World War (a new Constitution replaced that of 1885 and extended franchise to all adults including women who were literate in any language spoken in the country). The elections in 1948, though not fully representative can be described as historical as around 90 percent of registered voters could cast their votes. This new Constitution encouraged people of the Indian origin, the majority of them constituting a working class, to be literate. It was during 1950s and early 1960s that the political activity got heightened and that led to formation of many political parties, mostly based on communal lines, for self government and independence of the country. Another new Constitution framed in 1958, for the first time introduced universal adult suffrage. Despite communal and ethnic riots, Mauritius attained independence on 12th March, 1968, with no major upheavals. Since then, it has upheld its democratic culture. Further, since independence, though the Constitution has witnessed some amendments but not substantial changes, yet it provides special provisions for the protection of the fundamental rights and freedom of the individual and does not permit any discrimination on the basis of race, place of origin, political opinions, colour, creed or sex. In short, Mauritius can pride itself to be a democratic country with a written Constitution, frequent free and fair elections, a British parliamentary form of government, a free press, an independent judiciary and well-organized trade unions. It is on these pillars that the democratic structure of this tiny nation has been built (Mohammedbhai (Foreword) in Dukhira, 2002).

In 1959, a new political outfit was formed by a section of Muslim community. This Party, the Committed Action Musulman (CAM) entered into an alliance with the Labour Party, which was headed by a British-trained Indo Mauritian doctor, Seewoosagur Ramgoolam, and fought the election for the pro-independence of the country. Another Hindu political outfit led by Sookdeo Bissoondoyal, (The Independent Forward Block (IFB)), also contested the election. The Parti Mauricien Social Democrate (PSMD) led by Gaetan Duval, pursued an ethnic campaign by mobilizing support of the Creole community, against the likely domination of Hindus in the political set up. This Party was against the independence of the country and vouched for continuation of the links with Britain. Labour Party won a decisive victory and Dr. Ramgoolam became Chief Minister in 1961. However, three years later, a ministerial system got introduced and he was appointed Prime Minister. But, the elections of 1963 were not without violence as these were heightened by a sense of communalism based on ethnic identity.

It was during this time, a number of Constitutional meetings were held in London against the rising unrest and tension among the ethnic groups within the country and the delegates made a clarion call for an electoral system that should adequately take care of minority representations, In the final Conference in 1965, a 'Best Loser' system was adopted, which guaranteed seats for minorities. The 1967 election, was a sort of representation on Independence. Muslim vote was observed to split as some members supported the pro-independence Movement while others supported the PMSD and IFB political outfits but the pro-independence Party led by Ramgoolam, won the election, with an absolute majority. However, the island witnessed a racial violence in January 1968, which originated in Port Louis and members of minority groups started emigrating to Australia, Europe, South Africa and Canada because it was being rumoured by Duval's PMSD that the "*Bateau langouti*" was en route to the island (Mauritians would be compelled to adopt Indian dresses). Further, the "Best Loser" system will institutionalise communalism through the ethnic identification of the candidates (Marin in Lal, 2007).

In this entire journey to freedom Movement, one person who stands taller than others is Sir Seewoosagur Ramgoolam. We need to make a special mention of him because of his qualities of head and heart. With the support of his elder brother and uncle, as his father died while he was young, Ramgoolam who belonged to a prosperous Bhuguth family, after the completion of his secondary education in Mauritius, went for his medical training in England. He returned to his homeland after more than a decade while he got his degree in Medicine but he was observed to be inspired by the Fabian Socialist values. An important member of Labour Party, he was appointed the first Prime Minister of independent Mauritius on March 12, 1968. Popularly known as "Chacha" and respected as a "father of the nation", he held this position for several years. During his tenure, he strived his best to evolve Mauritius as an emerging democratic welfare state through his policies and actions based on politics of accommodation in a multi-ethnic and religious tension ridden country. His major contributions include the introduction of free education at all levels and various other social welfare schemes for the needy and deserving people.

He opined that "man has emancipated himself from the laws of jungle by education and experience" and persuaded the British again to provide the people of Mauritius, facilities for the study of languages at school, which raise their pride, tradition and civilities (Dukhira, 2002).

Not only, he was an astute politician having shrewd understanding of the people and situations but also a great visionary as he realized that without making the fundamentals of education strong, the country shall not progress and achieve other developmental goals such as political, economic and social. As a politician, he always held tolerance and respect for others, a value that is significant in the Indian culture. That helped him to steer successfully his path of development of the island despite its ethnic diversity. Besides, he was observed to have complete identification with the people, especially in the villages, where he devoted his holidays to attend socio-cultural functions. He continued his parliamentary life from 1940 to 1982 as his Party lost then and he passed away on 15 December, 1985 as Governor General of Mauritius. A Samadhi and a memorial has been built in his honour at Pamplemousses Botanical Garden, where his body was cremated.

A historical account of freedom struggle given above clearly shows that people of the Indian origin, making a clarion call for the Independence of the country from the British colonists, must have confronted humiliations, insinuations, oppression, exploitation and discrimination of the worst order at their hands. Despite these, their dogged persistence and perseverance and tolerant attitude (tolerance is a great Indian value) fructified in making Mauritius an independent nation.

Electoral Politics: Gains and Pains of Democracy

Democracy, derives its roots from Greek term demokratia; "demos" indicating 'people' and "kratos" as "rules". As such, it denotes a political system in which the people and not monarchs or aristocrats, rule. However, the catchword **'the people'** is problematic in terms of who they are, kind of participation they can have and the conditions for their participation. We have representative, multi-party democracy, representative one party democracy and participatory or direct democracy. Though the 'original' type of democracy, that was found in ancient Greece is participatory democracy where decisions were taken in the community by those affected by them. Yet in modern societies, which practice multi-party representational democracy where all the adult population has right to vote at different levels, we have usually liberal democracies (Giddens, 1989).

In the west, the normal order of democracy was influenced by Christianity, which signified the identity of an individual and the civil society, as the basic premises of democratic decisions making. In that sense, religion was thought to provide meaning to social life and its ideology to induce individuals to conform to the existing social order or change it. However, in framing Mauritian Constitution, there is no importance attached to religion and people are supposed to rise above the primordial ties or associations of ethnicity.

In fact, the rule by the "people" is now widespread across the world as nearly 115 countries have adopted one form or the other of the democratic governance and of these, 81 countries have attained this transition only during the last two decades. However, the "rule by the people" in cultural sense does not hold good because it fails to act in the interests of all persons in an autonomous territorial state. This is the main drawback of democracy. It is reported that accountability, electoral legitimacy, Constitutional safeguards and functional institutions are the key pillars, which have universal acceptance of democracy (UNDP, 2002)

But, if liberty and equality are the basic aims of democracy, then all persons in the government must share alike to the utmost to achieve it. In fact, James S. Mills statement that representative democracies are "the grand discovery of all times" is remarkable.

Now, democracy is considered as an essential input for development since it can provide more efficient, open and accountable governments through a participative approach to have greater mobilization of the socio-economic groups, good governance through increased participation in institutions, decentralized power structure, freedom from discrimination, freedom of expression, respect for human rights and economic and social policies that are good for people. But democracy is not without pangs. Political systems committed to it, are seeking various permutations and combinations of many types in making governance workable in their respective systems by having different shades of the political, social, economic and cultural aspects in it but they do not find satisfactory arrangements. As observed, some democratic systems consider health and education as functions of income while others view these as functions of human rights. Besides, for certain social systems, the concentration of wealth in a few hands can coexist with an extreme poverty situation without affecting the fabric of democracy, while for others, democracy means elimination of extreme wealth as well as poverty (Somavia, 1981).

In the above backdrop, we need to analyse the gains and pains that the Mauritian Society had by adopting a parliamentary system of governance which aimed to provide freedom, equality and fraternity to its people irrespective of their age, sex, ethnic identities, religious adherences, racial and linguistic affiliations. Mauritius adopted the agreement reached at the London conference of September 1956 that adult sufferage and minority interests be safeguarded in the voting pattern as a form of electoral process. Besides, voting should be done along the Party lines to avoid communalism. It was also agreed that Mauritius would follow the electoral system of "first-past-the post" as adopted in the United Kingdom and passed on to the former British colonies to accommodate minority groups.

However, the proposal for proportional representation was abandoned and an electoral boundaries commission was appointed.,which on its visit examined the recommendation of different parties (Labour Party, CAM, IFB and PMSD) and after debate, its report was adopted in 1958 in which inter-alia, it prescribed forty single-member constituencies. On 11th march, 1964, a new Constitution was published in a special edition of Government Gazette wherein the Legislative and the Executive Councils were re-named as the Legislative Assembly and the Council of Ministers. Later on, in its memorandum to the Secretary for the colonies at the time of September 1965 Constitutional conference in London, Mauritian Labour Party stressed on the early grant of independence and pressed for franchise for all those who were 18 years old and above, collective ministerial responsibility, a leader of opposition, an independent service commission with executive powers, requirement of two-thirds of all legislators for amending the Constitution and a chapter in the Constitution on fundamental rights. On 30th December 1965, the Secretary of State for colonies appointed a Commission to make recommendations for an electoral system along with method of allocating seats in the legislature that suits Mauritius the most and the boundaries of the electoral constituencies.

This commission headed by Sir G. Harold Banwell, in its report suggested twenty constituencies, each returning three members on the main land and two member constituency for Rodrigues, a dominion of Mauritius. The voting was to be done on the basis of block system (voting for three candidates in Mauritius and two for Rodrigues) and a suggestion for the creation of an Electoral Commission was also given. Besides, the percentage of votes polled by each Party was to determine the number of seats in the Legislative Assembly, referred to as the corrective system. This corrective system as a part of report was vehemently opposed by all parties except PMSD, which endorsed it fully. Consequently, because of the consistent opposition, the British regime sent Assistant Parliamentary Secretary John Stone House to Mauritius and after discussion with all parties, substituted the corrective system by one based on "eight best loser system". In view of this, the Legislature Assembly was to have in all a total of 70 MPs (Members of Parliament), out of which sixty were to be elected in twenty, (three member) constituencies on the island of Mauritius and two in Rodrigues and up to eight nominees chosen from among the defeated candidates on the bases of community and the best results obtained in the general election Party-wise (Best loser system). This electoral arrangement is still in practice (Dukhira, 2002).

The electoral system evolved within the parliamentary system of democratic governance,is tried and tested over the years to pursue planned interventions for the development of Mauritius. People on the island through voting system chose their representatives, depending upon their allegiance to a particular political Party of their respective ideological underpinning. Democracy provided them an opportunity to raise voices in support of their representatives or oppose others whom they thought, were not able to fulfil their needs and wants. The electoral system also provided freedom of expression or speech to many of them to give vent to their feelings, motivations and desires. They also got better exposure to the local as well as outside world because of Mass Media, both printed and non-printed like radio, television and cable networks. Besides, the institutions- financial, economic, social, cultural, along with non-governmental organizations, provided them with basic amenities and social-welfare measures such as education, health care, old-age pension and security arrangements. Their participation in the electoral process built up confidence in them and they felt emancipated from the feudal system dominated by sugar barons and could take care of themselves and their families in a more befitting manner than before. Debates, discussions on issues that concern citizens have brought in greater enlightenment to most of the people. They have now better aspirations for the education and employment of their children. Most important is, that people now on their part can take decisions on matters that concern them. These are some of the gains that people may visualize in democratic governance.

Though, democracy is considered conducive for development purposes as one can sort out issues connected with the needs or problems of the people, yet the capital mode pursued in the development strategies of Mauritius, has resulted in further concentration of wealth in a few hands, raising income disparities between individuals and ethnic groups, widening of gaps in lifestyles of rich and poor and in urban and rural regions, exclusive than inclusive development of people as many persons and groups have been marginalized, raising unemployment especially among the educated and school drop-out youth, increasing crime rates as a consequence of expansion of tourism on the island (theft, dacoity, murder, rape and prostitution) and environmental hazards caused by carbon emissions of increased vehicular traffic, filth and garbage spread along the beaches by large number of tourist inflows and floods caused by heavy rains. Over the years, the ministerial system as a part of parliamentary form of governance has also resulted in corrupt and sharp practices pursued by politicians and bureaucrats. There appears some collusion between political and economic elites in the globalisation of social and economic life. As Mauritius is an export-oriented economy due to its limited domestic market; in its effort to be a part of globalisation process, it has experienced gains for a few and pains for many. Notwithstanding the pains inflicted on the large majority of population, it has continued with its commitment to democracy despite criticism of its functioning in print and non-print media and among more militant groups and vocal individuals, who have, from time to time, voiced their dissents, protests and insinuations against its democratic governance through electoral system.

In certain quarters, there is a demand being made by certain individuals and groups to effect electoral reforms for making democracy inclusive in the country. The electoral system was inherited from colonial Britain and it was subjected for examination by an expert (popularly known as Sachs report) group. After careful study by a parliamentary Select Committee, it was unanimously agreed that the prevailing electoral system needs an immediate review. The main problem encountered with the present electoral system is the First-Past-the-Post/Block-Vote (FPTP-BV), which has given rise to a lopsided parliament as it fails to take into account the choice of the voters. It is argued that the opposition Party is generally significantly un-represented because a Party that gets a little over 50 percent of votes, can often win all the parliamentary seats. There is a need to have an electoral system that should suit to the diverse composition of Mauritian population (gender, ethnic and religion) to make politics inclusive to the extent possible by having fair representation of all communities and groups including physically handicapped, as the right to make political choice is a fundamental human right of all. Besides, the electoral system is insensitive to the gender composition of population. As a consequence of that, both within the political outfits and in the parliament itself, women are grossly under represented. Though the situation in recent elections for women is encouraging as the number of seats occupied by them in Parliament has increased, yet it exhibits only a token presence. There is an immediate need to have greater involvement of them at all levels of political life, national as well as local self-government.

The above issues were debated in a workshop (Electoral Reform-Moving towards an Inclusive Democracy held on February 17-18, 2006, at the University of Mauritius, Reduit), where it was argued that without necessary Constitutional and legal changes, the electoral reform by itself might not act as a panacea for all the ills of democratic governance. Some of the recommendations inter-alia included strengthening of power of Electoral supervisory and Boundaries Commissions, code of conduct for political parties and politicians, prevention of abuse by the outside government, setting clear rules and regulations for public institutions and their officials prior to and during elections, making voter registration an ongoing process, electronic voting, non-littering of environment during elections, funding of political parties, rationalization of terms of office of the President in the Republic to correspond with the life of the given Parliament and making the electoral reforms not only for the Legislature elections but also for the Municipal and District level elections (Institute of Social Development and Peace, Conference Proceedings, 2006)

The "Best Loser System" under Block voting is a debatable issue between the ruling formation and its opponents. This may not find an easy solution as those in rule have an edge over the opposition, to take advantage of the election outcome by resorting to manipulating and manoeuvring actions. Instead of democracy providing a negotiated set of understandings by having communication along horizontal lines between political parties (those in rule and in opposition), it twists the communication pattern along vertical lines where the ruling groups follow the dubious ways and means to scuttle, postpone or stall decisions on matters concerning all through actions which they find instrumental to their advantage. This is another pain that democracy through its electoral system inflicts on the subjects.

Political Arithmetic: Entrenched Ethnicity Coalition Politics

Mauritius, no doubt, as a part of the market and export-oriented economy, is emerging fast as an accelerating force towards globalisation. Yet increasing political conflicts, inadequate institutional apparatus, non-prioritisation of issues and objectives, local and regional contexts and vested interest of individuals and non-cooperation among some persons, pose challenges for its full realization towards globalisation. It is observed that cultural groupings in the developed as well as in the developing nations are getting strengthened as a reaction to the fractured globalisation process. Besides, a strong cultural sensitivity to which all groups are subjected, has resulted in the resurgence of ethnic identities across the globe.

To understand culture comprehensively, we need to look at it from "culture for the people" and " culture by the people" (Hammel, 1990). In the former sense, it plays a deterministic role to establish behaviour patterns among people by indoctrination of norms and values while in the latter sense, as rational human beings, men create meaningful responses from the available options to generate behaviour patterns suitable to emerging settings, situations and contexts. In the globalisation process "culture by the people" gets limited to a small section of the population and because of its weak instrumentalities and expressiveness, it cannot influence the majority of population whereas "culture for the people" accommodates and comforts all those who feel marginalized, alienated, pauperised, disprivileged and discriminated by the market economic forces, triggered by the globalisation process. As a reaction to this, most of the people because of cultural sensitivity, find human symbols and codes created by them for their social existence as more security prone than market settings. As such, ethnic identities based on cultural grouping and primordial ties such as territory, language, caste, kinship, religion etc. have become more pronounced in the post modern era. (Mehta, 1999).

Mauritius is not an exception, and there is a renewed strengthening of ethnic identities in the electoral system for power holding under democratic governance. Cultural pluralism having distinctive institutional framework based on a different set of beliefs, values, ethics, mores and actions for each of the ethnic group within a territorial population, needs to be understood for analysing the power structure or sharing of power between the significant cultural groups in the community or society. Certain cliques, cleavages, schisms or factions get formed in the society and at times it becomes necessary to have the convergence of interests of these to hold on power through shared interests to effect decisions that benefit not one group but some groups vis-à-vis the others. As such, they tend to form a coalition between themselves against the group or groups opposing them in their struggle to hold on to power structure. In this process, a political arithmetic becomes essential to coordinate the activities of one group with that of the other to have a "win-win" situation against the other group or groups who are competing to capture power in the community. As a consequence, coalition politics, assumes not only sufficient but necessary condition for holding on to power structure as by itself, one group may find it weak in controlling or influencing the decision making process affecting larger conglomeration of people.

The proverbial expression "politics makes strange bed fellows" exhibits a kind of surprise to all of us when we observe some new coalitions or alliances of men formed against our expectation based on the past knowledge of the participants in a community setting. Simmel ((1902-1970), 1950) opines that in a triad situation (three member interacting), two are in conflict with each other while the third either mediates between them or draws comfort and advantage from the conflict. It is argued by some social scientists while basing their assumption on the above proposition, that any triad tends to split into a coalition of two and a third one gets excluded. It is observed that a coalition gets formed if participants use their resources (a resource being a critical quantity of some weight that may hold two or more parties to determine the outcome of a decision) jointly to determine the outcome. But not all situations which use resources to affect the outcome of a decision lead to a coalition formation. In situations involving more than two parties, the research evidence suggests that coalition may take place only "within the context of mixed motive, n-person games, in which both conflict and common interest are simultaneously present, and must govern the courses of action chosen". There is hardly any chance that the outcome would bring greatest possible return to all players at one go. However, there is always a possibility that at least two of the players may fair better if they join hands to pool their resources.

We may look at the three main theories of coalition formation. One is minimum resource theory that highlights that a coalition will get formed even if the total resources are as small as possible but still sufficient enough to affect the formation. This is guided by the principle of parity norm based on distributive justice as each man, in exchange relations with another, expects that the net rewards or profits should be in proportion to his investments. The second theory of minimum power is based on the number of times a player becomes the pivotal member and is able to turn an insufficient coalition into a winning one. The third theory of coalition formation, (anti-competitive theory) focuses on the fact that players in the coalition situation do not want to compete with each other; rather they are keen to preserve social relationships between the groups. The coalition in such a situation gets formed along the laws of least resistance, which may be designed as a relation that exists between players who if combined, would have no problems in regard to dividing the gains. No doubt, as per parity norm or the pivotal power principle, the players need not bargain if the resources or power dimensions are unequal but in actual situation, one principle may invoke the other. However, in reality, when resources are unequal, bargaining of some kind will take place between the groups. All the three theories of coalition formation are relevant in different situations and need to be considered while analysing the political arithmetic to capture power or hold on to the power affecting the decision making process. Basically, a theory on coalition formation should be able to predict as to who will combine with whom and how they will divide the proceeds by obtaining a simple majority.

In essence, coalition means "a joint use of resources to determine the outcome of a decision in a mixed motive situation involving more than-two units". (Gamson, 1968).

In the above backdrop, one needs to analyse the coalition politics in Mauritius, which is in vogue since its independence on 12th March 1968 when it became a sovereign independent state among the Commonwealth nations with Queen of England as its head of State. However, the general elections of 1963 and 1967 in the pre-independent era assume significance as these paved the way to independence. Both these elections were fought by the political parties namely Labour Party (LP), Independent Forward Block (IFB) and the Parti Mauricien Socialist Democrate (PMSD) along ethnic lines. But in 1967, LP was supported by other two parties IFB and All Mauritian Hindu Congress (AMHC), along with the Muslim Party known as Committed Action Musulman (CAM) to fight PMSD which opposed the independence of the nation pursued jointly by the united Indo-Mauritian groups. The Labour Party and its allies were able to obtain 54 percent of the votes and secured 43 of the total 70 seats. Since independence, Mauritius has held eight general elections. All except one were fought between two coalitions.

The elections of 1976 was a three cornered one. In all the post independent elections, in as many as seven, namely 1982, 1983, 1987, 1995, 2000 and 2005, alliances were formed before elections while in 1976, a coalition was formed after the elections (an alliance is formed before election while a coalition is referred to an arrangement between parties after the election).

Before, we take up the coalition formation for various elections in the post independent era, we need to examine the ethnic composition of population on the island. Broadly, half the population constitutes persons of the Hindu religious stock (of these, nearly 40 percent are Hindi or Bhojpuri speaking, about 5 percent are Tamil speaking, nearly 3 percent are Marathi speaking, 2 percent or so, are Telugu speaking and about 1 percent may be Gujarati speaking), nearly one third, mainly Creoles are Christians (most of them are Catholic), 17 percent or so follow Islam and a very small proportion, around 3 percent or so are of Chinese origin (most of them are also of Christian faith) Though, English is the country's official language,yet French serves as a lingua franca but the most widespread vernacular dialect in vogue or in use is Creole, a hybrid language, a sort of brokèn French with words even from Bhojpuri, Tamil, Telugu, Urdu and other Indian languages like Marathi. As on 2000, nearly 70.1 percent of people speak Creole only at home while 12.1 percent speak Bhojpuri, French is spoken by 3.4 percent people at home, English is spoken by 0.3 percent, Chinese by 0.7 percent, Hindi by 0.6 percent, Marathi by 0.2 percent, Tamil by 0.3 percent, Telugu by 0.2 percent, Urdu by 0.1 percent while 12 percent people at home speak a combination of languages as a part of other category (Mauritius, Housing and Population Census, 2002).

Further, the Hindus have been divided vertically along caste lines, (The Brahmins and Kshatriyas constitute a small apex of population while the bulk of the Hindi population is composed of the Vaishya Varna while Shudras are also fairly well represented). Besides, there are religious sects among the Hindus as well as among the Muslims, the prominent among the Hindus are Santanists and Arya Samajists while those among Muslims are Shias and Sunnies. Almost all castes and sects that exist in India have their reinforcements on the island.

In view of the above, let us look at the process of coalition politics to capture power in the post-independence of the country. It appears that with the passage of time, the political parties abandoned their ideological underpinnings and acquired power to manage the affairs of this island nation by concentrating on the pivotal power of the member of the political Party who could pull other members with them by providing least resistance in the formation of the coalition to have a win-win situation against the opposition irrespective of the ideological differences, if valued at all. The first election of 1976 held in the post independent era is a testimony of the above statement (incidentally, one of the authors Shiv R. Mehta was an eye witness to this election). Ramgoolam who became the first Prime Minister of Independent Mauritius had conviction in Fabian Style socialism and to create equal opportunities for all, he favoured the creation of a welfare state and championed for free education on the island. But, because of political compulsion to appease various groups of multi ethnic community, he had no option but to include in his cabinet individuals having diverse interests who soon acquired unsavoury reputations for graft. This legacy has been passed on to all coalition partners in the subsequent elections who became managers of running the respective governments. Even now, the paramount significance is accorded to ethnicity than meritocracy. This has till date become a stumbling block to the effective governance in Mauritius. Fox (1966) has rightly pointed out that in traditional or quasi traditional societies which have a heavy input of primordial ties based on kinship-family, language or religion complex, ethnicity tends to prevail upon bureaucratic rationally based organizations in matter of recruitment of personnel. The merit of an individual often gets relegated or brushed aside. In other words, "who knows whom" and "show me the person, I show the rule" become the set ethos of administration.

Before the general election of 1976, against the ethnic-based politics and corruption, a Club of etudiants militants was formed in Mauritius which culminated later on, into the formation of the Mouvement Militant Mauricien (MMM), headed by a Franco-Mauritian graduate (Ideologically, a French Marxist who wooed the working class (Trade Unions of local workers and others) and the young of the island to the radical ideas of his newly created Party. A general strike was provoked by this Party in 1971 when the Mauritian economy was moving ahead because of creation of Export Processing Zone (EPZ) and diversifying into tourism sector. Though, the MMM started as anti-communal group, in 1976 election, it fielded candidates, keeping in view the ethnic composition of Constituencies, thus consolidating the politics of patronage that had dominated since independence. However, minorities in this election voted overwhelmingly for the MMM, indicating that the nationalist approach beyond the ethnic solidarities was better for the governance of the Mauritius nation-state. If we take into account the results of 1976 election, it was apparent that the MMM had almost won the election. The post independent Party (MMM) got 30 seats whereas the Labour Party in alliance with CAM got only 25 seats. The PMSD, an anti independent Party, was reduced to third place with 7 seats only (The nominated seats were shared, 3 Labour Party, one PMSD and 4 MMM) All other political outfits based on communal, religious or kinship basis were wiped out completely, but the caste or kinship factor was observed to play up in this election. Interestingly, Ramgoolam as head of the Labour Party wooed his one time opponent for Independence, Gaetan Duval, the leader of PMSD, to forge an alliance with him to keep out the MMM out of the power structure and form a government. The MMM leader Paul Berenger had no option but to sit in the opposition. This is where pivotal power theory holds good for the formation of coalition led government (Marin in Lal, 2007, Kadima and Kasenally, 2005, Mehta, 1981).

It was a weak coalition government headed by Ramgoolam as it was based on "partners as strange bed fellows". Despite censure motions on two occasions (1979 and 1980), it survived because of defections from the MMM Party for opportunistic reasons. Economic difficulties because of two devaluations imposed by IMF (International Monetary Fund) and corruption menaces denounced by a Commission of enquiry further enhanced the weakening of the Labour Party. In a furry, it expelled three of its national Assembly members who formed a new Party, Parti Socialiste Mauricien (PSM) led by Harish Bodhoo. This new political formation allied with other leaders and was responsible for the fall of Labour Party in 1982 general election, which saw some interesting ethnic combinations in politics. With a weakened LP, the MMM, despite its chances of sweeping the elections of 1982 was wary of the Hindu community, as they had the assured support of Muslim and the Creole community. In its nervousness, the MMM leadership entered into an alliance with the new PSM Party and it was agreed upon that in the event, the election was won, Anerood Jugnauth would be made the Prime Minister. This diluted the non-communal class-based image of MMM. However, the MMM and the PSM alliance swept this election and secured 60 seats while 2 seats each were secured by Parti D'Alliance National (Labour + Muslim Action Committee and dissenting PMSD members) and PMSD. But this political marriage did not last long between the MMM and PMSD due to dispute about the status of the Creole language and the stringent economic policies proposed by Paul Berenger, then Finance Minister under Jugnauth leadership. Jugnauth seized the opportunity to readily form a new political Party, Mouvement Socialiste Mauricien (MSM) after the breakdown of coalition government in nine months or so.

A fresh election was held in 1983, which saw the reunion of the Hindu community and entrenched politics of ethnicity. MSM led by Jugnauth, wooed LP and even PMSD which he had kept out in his early coalition government to confront the MMM. A similar combination of political outfits was followed even in 1987 elections. It is interesting to observe that both in 1983 and 1987 elections despite MMM Party securing a high proportion of votes, it could secure 22 and 24 seats respectively in these elections while the coalition led by Jugnauth got 46 and 44 seats. These elections also showed a new trend based on geographical location as the MMM had its constituencies represented predominantly in urban areas having concentration of the Muslim and Creole community while MSM and LP dominated the rural areas where there was a predominance of the Hindu community. However, in these political coalitions, Labour Party was anti-competitive and was providing the norm of least residence and remained at the receiving end. It got split due to sacking of one of its eminent leader (Satcam Boolell) while the split members joined the MSM Party. There was political instability observed from 1983 to 1986, the main reason attributed for that was the corruption within the government as evidenced by arrest of four MPs of the coalition government (one of them was caught with 20 kg of heroin in his luggage at Amsterdam Airport). One of the main partners, Harish Boodhoo resigned, after he levelled charges of corruption against Jugnauth. There was upsurge of resignations and defections, and that compelled Jugnauth to get back to Boollel of LP for support to survive his government. Ironically, the person who was dumped by him came to his rescue. (Kadima and Kasenally, 2005).

In 1989, the LP was making efforts to rebuild its strength after its debacle in 1982, so it entered into dialogue and discussion with other groups while following the minimum resource theory of coalition having parity norm. However, the discussions between LP and MMM, MMM and MSM and LP and MSM churned out a coalition strategy between the MSM and the MMM. The MMM, one time opponent was invited to join the government while LP had no option but to leave the coalition by mid 1990.

Anticipating a landslide victory, the coalition led by the MSM and the MMM, called for general election, a year ahead of the scheduled time. The reconstituted militant group was confident of victory as the LP with a new leader at the helm of affairs, Dr. Navin Ramgoolam (son of Sir Seewoosagur Ramgoolam) and the PMSD had weakened their locus-standi. They swept the 1991 election by securing 57 seats and 56.3 percent of popular votes. But this coalition government had a short life as a split was caused in MMM by Prem Nababsingh who formed a new Party, "the Renouveau Militant Mauricien" (RMM). With his supporters, he continued with the government while Berenger and his followers, sat in the opposition. By 1995, in the next general elections, Jugnauth had managed to retain his Prime Ministership for nearly 13 years and his Party, the MSP had masterminded a series of alliances since 1983 based on ethnic arithmetic. However, in 1995 elections, the Labour Party supported by the MMM wiped out the combination of the MSM and RMM by securing 60 seats (63.7 percent votes) in an absolute manner (zero seat) while others got six seats. In this election, the socialist slant of Labour Party and that of MMM, (radical political outfit) was lost.

They based their coalition on the minimum resource theory having parity principle, to hold on to the power. But, in the 2000 general election, it was again a complete turn about for the militant group as they joined hands again with MSM, to capture 58 seats while 8 seats were shared by the

LP and Parti Mauricien Xavier Duval (a split group of PMSD). This coalition (MSM and MMM) had its basis on the pivotal power of the members in each of the political parties and they seem to have agreed to parity norm of sharing the outcome of the decisions taken by them having mixed motives. It was agreed that the term of Prime Minister will be split into two halves, and the coalition leader of each party by turn, shall assume the office and each Party shall secure 30 parliamentary seats. This pre-electoral accord between the two political parties was remarkable in the sense that for the first time, it provided a Franco-Mauritian (Paul Beranger, a French White) to hold the office of Prime Minister in a totally predominant Hindu majority group on the island. So far, the top leadership has always been held by a person of a particular sub-group from the Hindu community. Coalition politics has come to stay in Mauritius as the ethnic diversity has been handled with dynamism by the leaders of the political parties to capture power. There is a consensus developed in them that we need to accommodate the diverse population as all of them give precedence to ethnic identity over the ideological tones. All parties are making a clarion call for social justice, sustainable and equitable development and a people oriented strategy. But, women representation in coalition politics is not given its due attention because of intra-Party competition faced by them by the more aggressive male colleagues. Another weak aspect of Mauritian coalition politics is that there is hardly any law to govern them. They need to be registered and their objective, duration and agreement should be made public. Further a flexible approach should be followed in realizing them (Kadima and Kasenally, 2005)

Before, we make an analysis of 2005 general election, it may be appropriate to examine the basis on which the

MSM and the MMM joined hands in 2000 election. It is reported that in February 1999, serious riots broke out when the popular Rastafarian singer Kaya, was imprisoned for possessing marijuana and he died in the police custody. The police failed to control the riots as the looting became widespread and the young Hindu militants took revenge for the Creole-inspired revolt by attacking and burning homes of Creoles in the Hindu dominated towns and villages. In an atmosphere of insecurity and general disillusionment, there emerged a new alliance of the MSM and MMM, and a power sharing formula got evolved between Jugnauth and Berenger. Voters thought that by making a non-Hindu as a Prime Minister, the ethnic deadlock over political appointment would be broken and a new era of meritocracy will usher in. However, this could not become a reality and Jugnauth,after his term, was made President and his son started nursing his Party. There has been continuation of communalization of political and socio-cultural organizations and that inspired the resurgent Labour Party to go in for the 2005 election on the anti-communal plank (Marin in Lal, 2005).

The election of 2005 again brought Navin Ramgoolam, the pivotal leader of the LP into saddle of power while Berenger, the MMM leader occupied the opposition chair. Jugnauth was blamed by a large majority of the Hindus, for passing on the power to a White (Berenger) and called it a return of European Colonialism. People of the upper castes, the Brahmins and Kshatriyas among the Hindus, were also annoyed with Jugnauth for allowing the non-Brahmin or lower caste priests to officiate in the Hindu temples. The case against the upper caste priests in the court of justice was fought by Sir Robin Ghurburrun, a Shudra by Caste. He championed the cause of priests of his caste groups to be installed in the temples. These developments weakened the stature of Jugnauth and his son, who was holding the reign of his Party. This enlarged the Labour Party base and with the help of smaller parties of Hindu faith, (a higher proportion of Tamils, Marathi and Telugu linguistic groups) and social solidarity group of the Muslims, it could form a government. The other coalition partner was the PMSD who got 7 seats and together the Labour Party coalition could obtain 38 seats while the MSM/MMM got only 32 seats. (Doolooa, 2007; Bertelsmann Stiftung BTI2008, Report, 2007)..

On our recent visit to Mauritius (January to May 2008), it was observed that the present Prime Minister Dr. Navin Ramgoolam had learnt the craft of managing politics in this complex ethnic ridden island nation by having three Deputy Prime Ministers drawn from the Muslim, Tamil and White Christian communities respectively, thus balancing the act of pulling through the coalition groups, hopefully to the next general elections, scheduled for 2010. The leader of the opposition Paul Berenger and his supporters have been observed, as witnessed on the Parliamentary debates telecast on Mauritius Television network, to corner the ruling coalitions on issues of food crisis, rising unemployment and poverty, environmental hazards and issues related to sharp and corrupt practices. Ahead of next election, coalition groups belonging to various ethnic combinations based on caste, class, religion, language, region (rural and urban inhabitants) have started hobnobbing with the political outfits of different hues and shades to enter into the power domain. As a reaction to one such move, Prime Minister Navin Ramgoolam had to sack one of his Ministers who was a partner in the coalition government. Further, on the Labour Day, on 1st May, all the major political parties had carried out huge rallies and the top leadership had raised allegations against each other's Party achievements or accomplishments.

However, these were held with discipline and without any untoward incident. But these rallies were indicative of the show of strength for the respective political outfits and a sort of preparation for the forthcoming elections in 2010.

Mauritian nation is politically vibrant and may serve as a laboratory for analyzing a coalition led political system. After making a succinct presentation of election outcomes in the post independent era, it may be worth examining the processes of coalition formation and the factors associated with the leadership structure thrown up by them. One significant observation is that barring 1976 election, all other elections were held with the prior formation of the alliances between the significant political groups. It is apparent from this that the leaders leading various alliance formations, were not bothered about ideological beliefs upheld by their respective parties but their one point goal was to capture or hold on to power, even if they have to float the parity norm advocated by minimum resource theory of coalition or act in an anticompetitive manner by providing least resistance to the major partner at the helm of affairs. Most of these coalitions in and during the election time are formed around members of respective parties who hold pivotal powers with them.

Thus, the pivotal power of a member becomes the central causal factor for the formation of coalition. This brings a paradigm shift in leadership structure as instead of being ideological based, it gets determined by the personality structure of individuals. It is in this sense that the "trait" or "great man" theory of leadership becomes significant than the functional theory that advocates satisfaction of needs and wants of the group by the leader for his or her legitimacy and continuity based on his or her ideological underpinning. However, the satisfaction of group goals or the achievement of the same by the leader cannot be ignored completely as these do contribute significantly in elevating a person to the leadership status.

Another significant observation in regard to the coalition formation and emergence of leadership is related to situational contingency thrown up by the electoral system adopted in the country. Apart from the diverse composition of the population along ethnic lines based on religion, region, caste, class, family- kinship complex and language, which provides sufficient opportunities to provide situations in social and political spaces to align groups together, the "best loser system" adopted in the Parliamentary system of governance gives an adequate chance or provides a situation that can be exploited to one's advantage by the coalition formation of a particular political Party. As such, the situational theory of leadership which states that the situation in which the group is placed, throws up chances for an individual to get into the leadership positions also holds good. In fact, leadership is the property of the group and as group structure changes; the leadership also tends to change (Homans 1950, Cartwright and Zander, 1956, Mehta, 1972)

In certain quarters in Mauritius, there is hue and cry raised against the "Best Loser System" and a voice is being raised for proportional representation of groups in the electoral system but this proposal is not acceptable to many who manage their chances of winning the election by capturing the power on this "Best Loser System" as it is believed that this procedure guarantees seats for the minorities. This is a debatable issue and needs consideration as a part of electoral reform being envisaged. Even, for fair women representation in Parliament, the proportional representation method may enhance their presence and visibility in the Assembly.

Further, because of ethnic diversity on the island, the political vote bank is influenced greatly by the religious, linguistic, caste, sect or class bases, One thing is certain that in Mauritian Politics, coalition as a medium to accommodate diverse groups as well as to throw up top leadership from a particular community, is going to stay and continue . Despite the fact that the Hindus as a community are divided along vertical and horizontal lines, no other individual from Muslim or Creole-Christian communities (Muslim nearly 17 percent and Creole/White Christians about 30 percent in population size) shall be in a position to hold on the apex leadership of the country, the main reason being the numerical dominance of the Hindu community over the others. Further, certain individuals within this community are economically dominant in their respective groups and by virtue of that, their family members are well-educated and enlightened members of the society. Also the freedom struggle against the colonists, threw up a number of committed leaders in this community who through dogged persistence and perseverance, acted as role models for the younger generations to uphold leadership positions. Moreover, the white population including Chinese are not more than three percent. They are interested only in trade and business and politics is not their cup of tea, but as business elites, they may influence the decision-making processes of the ruling governments. Black Creole/Christians, being backward and mainly not highly educated have slim chances of holding on to the power. However, the only white candidates, who dabbled in Mauritian politics were the conservatives led group of the politicians, Gaetan Duval (His son is now heading his legacy of PMSD) and the militant group leader Paul Berenger.

Berenger, a Franco Mauritian and a French Marxist, as a trade union leader, did venture to broaden his stronghold on the Indo-Mauritians by rallying around his radical ideas of social justice, equality and welfare and wooed the young population within the fold of his newly created political outfit but soon he lost his ideological direction and was swayed more so by his motive to capture the apex power structure. In this process, he èntered into coalition politics with the emerging Hindu leaders and in his four decades of political life, he managed to be a half-time Prime Minister with the support of Jugnauth Hindu base. His uprise in politics was supported largely by the Creole and white Christians but he climbed the ladder of political system only with the help of the Muslims who, by and large, are also backward and not highly educated. Muslims, strategically sit on the fence of politics and shift their allegiance to that group or combination that provides support and help them with some benefits. The situational contingency is what matters most to them. However, they are the key deciding factor in politics as many of them, over the years, have acquired business and trade acumen and become wealthy to dabble in the Mauritian Politics in the future.

A succinct analysis of election results in the post-independent era, pose a serious question for the political masters of the country, whether or not the political system can rise above the ethnic underpinnings and make a focus on the development of its people. The poverty ratio especially in the rural sector is growing fast and the wealth is getting concentrated in a few hands. No doubt, elections can become instrumental in providing alteration to the political parties in power game but Mauritius needs good governance by having an efficient administration of its resources for equitable distribution to all, to make inclusive development a reality. Is it possible to achieve it in an ethnic ridden nation of 1.2 million people, of which the Christians comprising of Chinese, Creoles and Franco-Mauritians are nearly one-third of it while the Hindus represent nearly half the population and the Muslims constitute about 17 percent of it. However, the Indo-Mauritians are not a homogeneous group as they are divided along regional, caste and religious lines. The major group among the Hindus is that of North Indian origin (mostly Bihari) and has the caste based divisions such as *Maraz; Babujee, Vaish and Ravived*, besides minority groups of Tamil, Telugu, Marathi and Gujarati. Marazs are Brahmins, Babujees are Kshatriyas but constitute a small proportion while Vaishs hold the key in electing a Prime Minister as this group is the largest one and *Ravived* as Shudras are fairly well represented in the caste hierarchy (the only exception was when Paul Berenger, a Franco-Mauritius, held Prime Ministership on sharing basis with Jugnauth). Even the Muslims among the Indo-Mauritians are divided into "Calcuttyas" and smaller minorities such as Surtees, Memons, Bohras, Khajas, Cokins and Anjounees (Marin in Lal, 2007).

In the light of the above composition, it is very difficult to make any prognosis about the Mauritian political system that has been checkered by the permutations and combinations of ethnic alliances cutting across the Party lines. However, a study of political parties and democracy in Mauritius, brought out that in the July 2005 general elections, 72 political parties got registered but the largest three parties which dominated the scene were Mouvement Militant Mauricien (MMM), the Labour Party (LP) and the Mouvement Socialiste Mauricien (MSM). Interestingly, each of these political outfits entered into alliance with one or the other at different times and exhibited their dominance.

No doubt, Mauritius has evolved a strong ballot culture but the first-past-the-post electoral system (Best Loser System) is not fair for indicating Party representation as there is a disproportion between the percentage of popular votes cast and the number of seats won in the Parliament. This needs a change but it is difficult to affect it because of vested interests of the Party in power. Further, it was revealed that the major political parties have leaning towards the socialist ideology and are guided by the Party Constitution. However, many members do not have knowledge of its contents. There is a well-developed internal Party structure, which follows a bottom-up approach in decision-making and the Party leaders have a say in selection, or nomination of candidates, party funding and information of coalition partners. But there are consultations done with other Party members. However, there is reluctance on their part to disclose information related to financial resources of the parties in race for elections. It is observed that though Mauritian Parliamentarians are fairly educated and professional in their fields, yet all of them are not fully familiar with the functioning of the Parliament and of political parties. There is a necessity for the voters to have reflective choices and the politicians to develop a culture of transparency and accountability to make Mauritius a more capable and inclusive nation-state to strengthen the democratic governance (Bunwaree and Kasenally, 2006).

If the above findings of the study are to be taken seriously for building up good governance on the island, then the nation must exhibit its secular credentials. Though the state in its Constitutional commitment has secularism as one of its tenets, yet in reality the society is bogged down by the religious dogmas. At every religious congregation of any faith, though the leaders speak for Mauritius to be one nation with distributive justice as its major goal, yet the platform provided by these religious organizations are used to make political speeches to woo voters for election purposes. This strengthens the entrenchment of ethnic identities and is anti-democratic for a nation that embraces democratic governance. Besides, there is a genuine need to root out graft and corruption from the political system. This has been caused mainly because of collusion of the economic elites who are obliged by the political masters to get the development projects or schemes and in lieu of that, make demands either in kind or cash. This is reflected by *Transparency International Corruption Perception Index's* Ranking of Mauritius at 42nd, out of 163 countries in 2006. This is testimony to the fact that corruption seems to be a serious problem (Bertelsmann Stiftung BTI, 2008, 2007)

Political apparatus in Mauritius should show transparency and accountability in its internal and external systems and address the emerging issues of poverty, unemployment among youth, food-production, milk production, environmental sustainability and human rights etc on a well informed basis to make development of the island people centered, cultural specific and local based than making a clarion call for high-end technology based activities having large investments from across the other regions of the world. This may prove counter-productive in the long run and the MNCs and TNCs, through the dubious mechanisms may cause economic bankruptcy. No doubt, Mauritian politicians are smart and intelligent and they have a knack of managing the affairs of the island by wooing meaningful investors, yet their total outward looking policies may not solve the problems of malnourishment, poverty, and unemployment, being increasingly felt and witnessed by its population.

Unlike Habermas remark in his *Theory of Communicative Action (1981, 1984)* that there is a coupling between the State (polity) and economy in a modern society, there appears some sort of uncoupling between them as a part of the "System" which interacts with "Life world" constituting the Private and Public Spheres. However, this uncoupling appears to be bridged between the political and economic elites through mutual negotiated understandings to share the cake of development. Because of complex Mauritian social structure involving various uncertainties, it may be difficult to make any forecast for the emergence of leadership structure in the near future. However, one thing is certain that irrespective of the compulsion of ethnic composition to enter into coalition politics, the leadership shall tend to crystallize in individuals having economic dominance within a particular ethnic group or groups or shall rest with those who have numerical dominance of their respective ethnic community or shall fall with those who take advantage of the situational opportunities thrown up by the changing social structure of this country.

Media, Non-Governmental and Welfare Organizations and Local Governance

Apart from Political apparatus, Judiciary and Executive institutions, media whether print or non-print (audio-visual) have always been the fourth pillar of democratic governance. Conscientization and sensitization of people through projected or non-projected media (News papers, magazines, Pamphlets) make them conscious and aware about the development issues, political and human rights, environmental hazards, growth and equity, women's right and gender problems, education, medical and health care, transport and communication problems etc. Media of communication is not only the reflection of a society but through the creation of images, visuals, projections, the media men and media-organizations can create new values among the people and move the society towards the desired direction. At least, if not possible to transform, media can act as a facilitator or accelerator of social change. In democracy, information revolution or communication revolution has been considered as a pre-requisite for development of a nation. Whether it is transmission of information or knowledge through Mechanical means, or it is Stimulus-Response syndrome in the Psychological space (now the emphasis is more on response rather on stimulus structure) or it is Empathy created to influence self or other or it is communication based on Pragmatics, that is, based on a day to day use of common language to build up an information system from outside and within the country, all these perspectives are basically aiming to develop an information or knowledge society.

Historically speaking, it is reported that on 13th January 1773, the first issue of *Annonees Affiches et Avis pour les colonies des iles de France de Bourbon* was published by Nicholas Lambert, as an official economic Journal. Later on, from 1832, *Le Cerneen* and *La Balance*, because of independent and free press, acted as influential players on the national scene, focusing debates for the political and economic emancipation of the population. At the time of our first visit (1975-1980), the print media was the monopoly of some persons who had the support of political groups or parties. The newspapers were in French except one which (Mauritius Times) had a part of English coverage. In fact, these were more or less political pamphlets, which voiced the opinion of the political parties to which they had developed allegiance. However, on our recent visit, the print media are not only confined to newspapers but also these include magazines of all types, special issues in English on Fridays and Sundays and are contributing significantly to nation building promoting consensus in favour of the development policies.

It is observed that Mauritian media throughout its 230 years of existence has played an important role in promoting participatory democracy. The literacy level, being high on the island and the advantage of knowledge of bi-linguism (French and English) has further hastened this process. People, by and large, are politically conscious and this is demonstrated by huge turnover of voters in the local and general elections. On an average, there is 66 percent of readership of newspapers, both dailies and periodicals and that is reported to be highest in the world. The credibility of Mauritian media is being strengthened as evidenced by 87 percent support of people holding good opinion in their favour, as revealed by Nelson-Taylor-Sofres survey. (Five years back, a survey indicated a 71 percent of "bonne opinion" (good opinion) for print media but for state owned television and radio, it was 52 percent). However, there is a need to evolve a consensus regarding professional code of ethics and a Press council to curb down arrogance, individualism and factionalism among Media Men and Media Organizations. (Claude de l'Estrac, 2005).

Though the first publication in Mauritius appeared in 1773 during the French regime, yet the press became free in 1831 during the British period. There was a Franco-Mauritian paper (La Cerneen) raising a voice against slavery, followed by La Balance and La Sentinell in 1843, which promoted the interest of non-white or coloured population. It is against this historical backdrop that the press got evolved into its present status. In the beginning of the 20th century, Indo-Mauritians, an important constituent of Mauritius, got organized and developed their own press. This was followed by Chinese who had their own newspaper.

The social and economic transformation as a response to 1929-30 crises, led to increased opposition to British rule. The Labour Party after its creation in 1936 supported this Movement by having involvement of the Hindu elites and the non-whites and the press became an essential instrument in their fight for their independence in 1968 and the status of Republic in 1991. It is observed that the Constitutional aspects are reflected in the organs of the press and the political parties also got organized along ethnic lines. The media in Mauritius pass through a kind of dualism between the state-controlled audio-visual service, which is used as a propaganda tool and a written press, trying to protect its autonomy, which acts as a political counterweight and represents public opinion. (The two major daily newspapers on the island: "Le Mauricien" was established in 1908 and "L' Express" in 1963. These are controlled by Creole bourgeoisie while a Hindu supported newspaper; "Mauritius Times" is published on weekly basis).

In late 80's and early 90's, things started changing and voices were raised to de-regulate the airwaves but it was only in 2001, such a change could be effected by promulgating a law for that. However, on 12th March, 2002 Radio One, Radio plus as well as Sky wave started broadcasting while the satellite dishes to receive foreign stations were legalized in 1994. Subsequently, an Independent Broadcasting Authority (IBA) was setup and four operators began satellite broadcasting. On the other hand, the Mauritius Broadcasting Corporation (MBC) maintained three Television channels and all its radio services. These developments enlarged the landscape of media in Mauritius by providing greater space for the expression of public opinion in the public sphere, thereby reinforcing democracy (Simonin, 2005).

Media Men, who manage Media Organizations, have the onerous responsibility of planning and programming the media contents and selecting the appropriate technologies for making communication more effective for development. As such, they need to possess professional competence, highly integrated personality, knowledgeability about local values and culture, imagination and sense of projection, sense of role commitment, honesty, purpose of sincerity, moral courage and willingness to work with people. These can be acquired both through professional "training" and "on the job" involvement. Further, rewards and facilities should be built into the organizational system to provide suitable working climate and generate greater commitment among the Media Men (Mehta, 1992).

In order to make development more people-oriented and decentralized, it would be apt to allow the micro-economic structure (social action groups, grass roots organizations or NGOs (Non-governmental organizations) to grow and fill the spaces left by the macro-economic structures of the State (Governmental and Political), in mobilizing men and money resources for the welfare of the people. These local organizations are the boon of a civil society and together with various media of communication can be instrumental in fostering political, economic and socio-cultural negotiations and understandings to arrive at a consensus of desired goals among the different partners (governmental and non-governmental) in the development initiatives. Often, these organizations are considered a threat to the macro structures but in fact, they need to be supported to enlarge the public sphere participation, to make development need-oriented, value-based and solidarity focused. We need to "conscientize" these micro level organizations for decision making in the development process. It is in this context that the "conscientization" perspective assumes significance within the communication perspectives for decentralized development planning. This can be followed by other development communication perspectives such as development of empathy, diffusion and adoption of innovations and the magic multiplying effect of electronic media to have deeper penetration into the way of life of people. The best way is to have media-mix of traditional and modern channels of communication by combining appropriately the folk and modern media, suitable to different situations. (Mehta, 1992).

In the early study on Mauritius (Mehta, 1981), the various organizations involved in welfare of the people at the village level were Village Councils, Youth Clubs, Social Welfare Organizations, such as "Malade Society", "Mutual Aid" and "Cooperative Society" and Religious Organizations like "Baitika", "Sabha", "Madrasa" and Anjuman Society" etc. Most of these welfare organizations were claiming a secular character but they had their roots in religious organizations. There is a preponderance of Hindu religious organizations followed by that of Muslim and Christian in that order. They have their roots in different cults, sects, religious beliefs and practices. Most of these organizations were religio-socio-cultural in nature and provided mutual aid, education, sports, debate, benevolent activities, consumer cooperatives, medical care and family planning facilities, recreational activities, solving local problem and ensuring cooperation among the villagers etc. Football appears to be national game and many clubs have emerged on the island which are active in promoting a healthy competition and discipline among the youth. These organizations are granted aid by the government to make them run smoothly but there is, at times, some friction among the members, a rivalry for leadership, a limited breadth of activities, lack of communication among the members and not so easy accessibility to these because of the distant locations. Some of these organizations because of limited funds at their disposal lack physical facilities and press the government for more grants.

A recent account of these organizations as given by Dukhira (2002), shows that they number around 4,500, out of which 540 are senior citizens' clubs recognized under the registration of Associations Act, 1978. Around 3000 of them are large organizations, having membership of more than 200 members, with assets over Rs .100,000 (One lakh) and an annual revenue exceeding Rs. 8000. (Political Parties,

Youth Clubs and Organizations covered under other incorporated laws are outside the domain of these organizations). Some of the leading Non-governmental Organizations that have contributed significantly for the welfare of the needy and deserving persons on the island are Mauritius Red Cross Society, St. John Ambulance, Rotary Club, the Lions Club, Giants International, Institute pour le development et le progress, Mauritius Cancer Society, Mauritius Mental Health Association, Foundation Es poir et. Development, Ecole power la solidarite' et al Justice, Ecole Complementaire, Arya Sabha (having 404 branches of which 153 are for women and 55 are youth wings, running 195 Hindi schools where classes are held on both week days in afternoons and Sundays), Hindi Pracharini Sabha (runs Hindi classes at 150 evening and 35 weekend schools), Mauritius Council of Social Services (an umbrella NGO to coordinate charitable activities, social health, education, relief for poverty or stress, and the Society for the Welfare of Deaf. Mauritius, being a welfare state not only provides free education and health but also social security benefits and housing, pensions, basic retirement benefits and subsidized rice and flour to its people. (Dukhira, 2002).

The fact that a large number of welfare organizations exist across the country, both in urban and rural areas, especially those of youth, should be a good case in point for mobilizing this huge resource for the development of the country (Mehta, 1981).

In regard to local administration and governance, Mauritius as a part of its Constitution, has provisions of District level administration, the urban centers or towns managed by Municipal Councils while the rural areas are governed by the Village Level Councils. Decentralization is a key to democratic governance as it encourages greater participation of people in the development initiatives. It is argued that centralization process has failed to help the poor and needy as that provides only exclusive development and render certain groups marginal, whereas decentralized administration by involving people at the local, or grass roots level, is bound to enhance the role commitment of all persons in different groups (Mehta, 1984).

In Mauritius, members of Village and Municipal Councils are elected, like those of National Assembly by virtue of the 'Representation of the Peoples Act'. The Council, especially in the townships offers a number of services and facilities apart from the Municipal Council of Port Louis, having 30 members and the four in Plaines Wilhems, having 24 members each. There is a two-tier local government for the rural areas. There are four District Councils and each except one (Black River in the West) has a membership of 36 persons and these are superimposed on 124 Village Councils, each having 12 members. At present, the Village Councils though elected directly and mandated with certain responsibilities are hardly effective, as they do not have resources of their own. However, the District Councils are elected indirectly and are politically unstable. The Village Council can replace if it likes, a representative only after one year. Further, unlike the urban authority, the District Council does not levy property tax or deliver construction permits. Moreover, it fails to perform even mandatory duties because of inadequate funds (Selex, 2007).

No doubt, Mauritius has a long history of local administration, beginning from French period through British regime to post-independence era, but even after four decades of independence, despite many reports for reforming it, no serious development has marked local administration, right from First Local Government Act of 1962 up to the latest one of 2003. Up to now, local government is not Constitutionally recognized. There is a tendency to centralize rather than decentralize local government as most of the decisions taken for it are with the approval of the Central government through the concerned Ministry (Decisions related to finance, job creation, international relationship or capital project). Political leaders must realize that local bodies play an important role in the socio-economic development of the country. As such, the financial grants to local authorities should not be conceived in terms of a privilege but as a right, as they are doing those tasks that should have been performed by the Central Government. (Maudarin, Selex, 2007).

The terms of office of Municipal and Village Councillors are of five years like that of Members of Parliament. But the District Council has indirect election where one representative of each Village Council of the area, is chosen in it and he or she can be replaced after one year. Further, the lord Mayor of Port-Louis, the Mayors of the other four townships and chairpersons of Village and District Councils are elected annually by the members, representing these organizations. They are also eligible to be re-elected. Village Council elections, which were due in 2002, were postponed for one year, awaiting the passing of a new Local Government Act (Dukhira, 2002).

Rural Development Unit established in 1974 within Ministry of Economic Planning and Development which was catering to the development of rural areas, was dissolved in 1980s and changed into National Development Unit to promote regional level development. The responsibility to develop the rural areas within the Village Council was passed on to the District Council. This tantamounted, to centralization rather than decentralization of local administration. Without autonomy in functioning of these local bodies especially related to financial matters, the local bodies will become ineffective. How can there be decentralization within the centralized system of administration? This structural inconsistency because of gaps between the expected and performed roles makes these local level institutions dysfunctional. In essence, they become a liability rather than an asset to the central administration. Reforms in local governance through transfer of funds and tasks related to the needs of the people of the area under the jurisdiction of local bodies need rapt attention of the politicians. Moreover, they should seriously reconsider reviving the Rural Development Unit to take into account, the growing unemployment and poverty on the island. Often, the urban areas get developed at the cost of rural and unless the process is reversed, one is bound to expect exclusive rather inclusive development of Mauritius.

References

Bunwaree, Sheila and Kasenally Roukaya (2005) (Eds) *Political Parties and Democracy in Mauritius*, Johannesburg. EISA, Research Report No. 19.

Bertelsmann, Stiftung BTI 2008 Report (2007), *Mauritius Country Report*, Gutersloh.

Claude de L'Estrac, Jean (2005) "The Role and Responsbiility of the Mauritian Media in Forging a Democratic Culture in Mauritius" in Kasenally, Roukaya and Bunwaree Sheilla (Eds) *Media and Democracy in an age of Transition*. Mauritius OSSREA: A Mauritius Chapter. pp. 20-24.

Cartwright, Dorwin and Zander, Alvin (1956) (Eds), *Group Dynamics: Research and Theory*. Evanston, Illinois, Row Paterson Co.

Dahl, Robert (1961), *Who Governs?* New Haven and London, Yale University Press.

Doolooa, Atma (2007), *Castes in Mauritius, The Future of Indians and Hinduism*, New Delhi, Star Publications Pvt. Ltd. (Published at Maharain Ltd., STE Anne Street, Central Flaq, Mauritius.)

Dukhira, Chit (2002) *History of Mauritius, Experiments in Democracy.* Mauritius, Quatre Bornos, Published by Chit Dukhira, 6, Avenue des Orchidees.

Fox, Robin (1966), *Kinship and Marriage*, N.Y. Penguin.

Gidden, Anthony (1989) *Sociology* Cambridge, Polity Press

Gamson William A (1968), "Coalition Formation" in David L. Sills (Ed.) *International Encyclopedia of Social Sciences*, N.Y. Macmillan Company and the Free Press. Vol. 1. pp. 529-534.

Hammel, E.A. (1990), "A Theory of Culture for Demography" *Population and Development Review* Vol. 16. No. 3

Homans, George C. (1950), "The Job of the Leader", *The Human Group.* New York, Harcourt, Brace and World Inc.

Hunter, Floyd (1963) *Community Power Structure*, N.Y. Anchor Books.

Institute of Social Development and Peace (2006) *Electoral Reform: Moving Towards An Inclusive Democracy. Proceedings of a Conference*, University of Mauritius, Mauritius, 17-18 Feb.

Kadima K. Denis and Kasenally Roukaya (2005), "The Formation, Collapse and Revival of Political Party Coalitions in Mauritius: Ethnic, Logic and Calculation at Play", *Journal of Election Studies*. Vol. 4. No. 1, pp. 133-164.

Lal, Brij (Marin in) (2007) (Ed.) "Mauritius" *The Encyclopedia of Indian Diaspora*, Singapore, University of Singapore. pp. 203-272.

Mohammadbhai, "Foreward" in Dukhira Chit (2002), *History of Mauritius, Experiments in Democracy*, Mauritius, Quatre Bornes, 6, Avenue des. Orehides.

Mauritius, Central Statistical Organization (2000) *Housing and Population Census.*

Maudarin Regina, (2007), "Message" "*Local Democracy in Mauritius, the Way Forward*", *Selex* (Unity and Development) Mauritius, Sumara and Co. Ltd. p.7.

Mehta, S.R. (1972) *Emerging Pattern of Rural Leadership*, New Delhi, Wiley Eastern Private Limited

Mehta, S.R. (1981), *Social Development in Mauritius: A Study on Rural Modernization in an Island Community*. New Delhi, Wiley Eastern Limited.

Mehta, S.R. (1984), *Rural Development Policies and Programmes: A Sociological Perspective*. New Delhi, Sage Publication.

Mehta, S.R. (1992), (Ed.) *Communication and Development: Issues and Perspectives*, Jaipur and New Delhi, Rawat Publications.

Mehta, S.R. (1999) *Dynamics of Development: A Sociological Perspective*, New Delhi, Gyan Publishing House.

Simonin, Jacky (2005), "Media and Democracy in the Islands of the Indian Ocean: Transnational Investigations and Typological Perspective" in Kasenally Roukaya and Bunwaree Sheila (Eds) *Media and Democracy in an age of Transition*, OSSREA Mauritius Chapter, Mauritius, Reduit.

Somavia, Juan (1981) "The Democratization of Communication: From Minority Social Monopoly to Majority Social Representation" *Development Dialogue*, Sweden, Dag Hammarskjold Foundation Vol. 2.

Simmel, George (1902-1917) (1950), *The Sociology of George Simmel*, Edited and translated by Kurt. H. Wolff, Glencoe, Illinois, Free Press (First Published in German).

5

Socio-Cultural Dynamics

Concept of Social Change

Change is the law of nature. Nothing remains static and everything is moving. In the dynamics of a phenomenon be it physical, social or cultural, one has to examine the moving forces to account for energizing of matter or mind. In physical sciences, dynamics would mean mechanism of treating motion in itself and of the motion of bodies under the influence of forces. However, the physical system is a closed one and we have exact laws postulated to explain motion (for example, in physics we have laws of motion and thermodynamics which explain motion in bodies and generation of energy respectively). Again in biological sciences, we have laws pertaining to genetic inheritance, which determine the shape and form of the body and Darwinian laws of natural selection of species for their adaptation to the environment. In short, in analyzing the dynamics of a system, we have to delineate the interacting forces that may result in the causation of a particular phenomenon This may be possible in the context of physical or biological systems but in a social system which is open rather than closed, it may be difficult to identify exact patterns of interaction between social actors because of varied complexities and uncertainties in it (Mehta, 1999).

Social and cultural aspects of human life are two sides of the same coin. For understanding human group, community or society, we need to understand the patterns of action and interactions between them. The action initiated by an individual either in a physical or social setting involves plurality of actors, minimum two to initiate effective communication between them. This gets regulated through norms, values and standards evolved by the group or society to direct the interactions towards pre-determined goals mutually decided by the members. This leads to the establishment of social relations. When these social relations over a period of time and within a social space become relatively stable or institutionalized into organizational arrangements for the fulfilment of societal needs, these can then be abstracted to delineate the social structure of the group or society (Mehta 1999).

There is a well-established linkage between culture and social structure of a society. In fact, there cannot be any society devoid of culture. In conservative sociological explanation, structure is represented by an anatomy while the culture depicts the physiological phenomena through veins and arteries of vital organs to make the body function in an equilibrium manner. This structural-functional dimension of social structure has been contested by the Marxian perspective, which explains relationship between society and culture in terms of base-superstructure analogy. However, Peterson (1976) suggests four types of relationship between the two. The first three are cultural autonomy, culture creates social structure (Idealism) and social structure creates culture (materialism). The fourth type of relationship which is more prominent today is the interdependence between culture and social structure. Culture in its early formulation was conceived as an identifier of behaviour in particular circumstances of time, place and social position. People tend to show consistency in their behaviour, thus depicting a cultural pattern. Culture has also been viewed as an expression whereby actors in the inter-actional framework become aware of the symbolic effect of their behaviours on other actors in social networks. Culture also means a negotiated set of understandings whereby the individuals choose these symbols (created and maintained by patterns of selection by actors and through innovations) from the available repertoire of behaviours that have some coherence and endurability over time (Hammel, 1990). Central to the concept of culture, are values which are either appetitive or normative in types or cognitive, affective and connotative in components and are in different levels of abstraction in the descending order; value, value orientation, attitude and opinion (Peterson, 1976).

In the context of Mauritius, it would be desirable to analyse the changes observed in the socio cultural life of people over a period of time, especially those observed during the last four decades since its independence. The major thrust will be to highlight the changes observed in ethnic and racial relationships besides those in social stratificational aspects especially related to caste and class dimensions. Further, a change in the language use is significant to be highlighted as language is basic to the transmission of values to the children in the family and school as a part of socialization processes. Changes in institutional arrangements related to Family, Marriage and Gender status are also important because of the development initiatives taken up by the state and that of natural phenomena in operation on the Island. The nation being multi-religious in its population has embraced democratic governance and secularism, as a value against religiosity, needs to be examined in the context of development of the society. In addition to the above, there is also globalizing of socio and cultural life of people, as the development of the society tends to become more outer than inner directed.

An attempt will be made to examine the above dimensions of social and cultural life of people for having better understanding of their movement from community to societal oriented way of life. It may be appropriate to make a mention here that there is no single theory coherent in nature that explains the phenomenon of social change. As such, various perspectives delineating change will be employed suitably to explain, the social, cultural, psychological, political and economic aspects. Change is being viewed as an alteration in any form, either in the structure or function of the social system whereas social structure of the system has been conceived as based on patterns of social action and interactions between actors to constitute structures embodying norms, values, cultural products and symbols.

Changes in Ethnic and Racial Relationships

Apparently, there does not appear any racial conflict between different racial groups such as White Europeans, African Creoles, Indo-Mauritians including both the Hindus and the Muslims and the Chinese Mongoloid. But underneath, there are biases and prejudices developed towards each racial group. It is observed that some element of distrust or jealousy persists between different ethnic groups. Yet no major clashes are reported between the Muslims and Hindus or Christians despite the population being pre-dominantly Indian. However, a certain amount of tension was observed between the fundamentalists belonging to the Hindu and Muslim communities at the time of India's war with Pakistan and Bangladesh. A conflict, however, took place among the people of Chinese origin in October 1956 when the two groups, one admirer of the Marshall Shek and the other favouring Mao-Tse-Tung came to blows in Port Louis and damaged the Chinese flag hurling on a school building. There was also a strong anti-Chinese feeling observed in the rural areas when China invaded India and some Chinese shops had to be closed down. However, the Chinese are not interested in local politics in Mauritius. They, mainly being shopkeepers, have to keep good terms with all the people to build up clientele of customers drawn from all the ethnic groups.

However, the 1965 racial tension, more of a political type, was simmering on the island and it culminated on the visit of Colonial Secretary (Anthony Greenwood) when the Mauritius Labour Party and Parti Mauricien held rural mass demonstrations in Port Louis. It was being rumoured that some Indian villagers were going to attack a village of African Creoles. In the remote villages in the South, a policeman and a Franco-Mauritian were murdered and 17 persons got injured. The state of emergency was proclaimed on May 14,1964, after order was restored on the island by the Cold-stream guards and it continued till July 31,1965. Again, just six weeks before the day of independence in 1968, more troops were brought in to manage racial rights in Port Louis between the Creoles and the Muslims; 25 people were killed and hundreds got injured. This was mainly due to electioneering campaign held in the previous year for the 1968 elections. This was so serious and a barbarous act by the Creoles on the Muslims that it compelled Muslim women to wear the traditional Hindu dress from being noticed by the Creole gangs. A lot of people lost their lives and it horrified all the inhabitants on the island. But this was a transitional phase that the country experienced before its independence.

However, in the post independence era, steps were taken by various respective governments to ensure co-operation and harmony between various racial and ethnic groups to develop a unified society (Doolooa, 2007).

But in the post independent era, again riots broke out in the year 1999 in the month of February when the popular Rasto-farin singer Kaya died in police custody after he was imprisoned for the possession of Marijuana drug. The looting became widespread and the young Hindu militants took revenge for the Creole directed revolt by attacking and burning homes of Creoles in the Hindu dominated towns and villages, as the police failed to control the riots.

Of various ethnic groups on the island, the most predominant is that of Indo-Mauritians including both the Hindus and the Muslims followed by the African Creoles, the Franco Mauritians and the Chinese. The Indo-Mauritians have contributed significantly in building up wealth in the nation through their hard work as most of them came to Mauritius in large numbers during the first hundred years of British rule. Indians by temperament were frugal and over the years, they saved a lot of money to acquire cultivable land in order to grow sugar and tea besides managing market gardens. Even today in Port Louis, Indian Muslims are the owners of huge buildings and they are successful traders. The community of the Indo-Mauritians has acquired education and necessary skills to manage the affairs of the island and it often looks towards India and Pakistan (Hindus towards India and Muslims towards Pakistan) for moral support and guidance. Efforts were directed by young men and women to teach Indian languages in every village and we have now an increasing number of Indian books and periodicals available in the market. In the 1930's, a fear was expressed that the entire Indo-Mauritian group may adopt Christianity but in the 1940s, there was an unprecedented revivalism of Indian religions and cultures. As an ethnic stock, the Hindus have always been referred as hardworking, committed and painstaking group. They braved themselves and worked courageously against heavy odds to save whatever they could do, to buy a cow or a piece of land to grow vegetables in the front or backyards. Through their meagre economic advancement, over a period of two to three decades, they were successful in taking over small estates and grow sugarcane on them. A large number of them established themselves as small planters and by virtue of that, they now own nearly one fourth of the country's sugar cane fields. Some of them did make large fortunes, but on the whole they could never attain higher status in the sugar industry (Doolooa, 2007).

The indentured labourers who immigrated to Mauritius from India also included a large number of Muslims. They also constitute nearly 17 percent of the population. Although, they are spread over the entire island, yet the majority of them are concentrated in urban centres or cities and are mostly engaged in trade and commerce. The rich Muslim merchants are concentrated in Port Louis and they own very large commercial concerns and buildings. They are also located in Beau Bassin and Rose Hill and are owning big houses. In winter months, they migrate with their families to their sea-side bungalows. Some of them are also residing in Vacoas/Phoenix. We have a substantial number of them who have attained professional status such as that of doctors, barristers, magistrates, diplomats and civil servants. Politically, they have been aligning themselves with the Hindus in the Labour Party during the 1950s but in the early 1970s they supported the post-independence created party MMM. In the last election of 2005, they were instrumental in the victory of Dr. Navin Ramgoolam of the Labour Party to head the government. The MMM is now trying hard to woo them back within their folds for the forthcoming election. Because of their large numerical size, it is not possible for any political outfit to ignore them as without their support, it may be difficult to form the government. Generally, as a shrewd political group, they sit on the edge and any political formation which offers them incentive of any kind, they switch over their loyalty to that group.

The Franco-Mauritians are the white settlers who came to the island during the French or British regime. In their mannerism and behaviour, they are still rigidly pursuing their religion and customary practices to uphold them as a separate ethnic group; mostly living in the secluded areas and not intermingling with people of other ethnic stocks. By and large, the economy of the nation is still in their hands and they own the sugar factories and the lands that produce the sugarcane. The French crown had given to all these settlers the land of the island, besides 50,000 acres. This enabled them to enrich themselves further by selling parts of the land to other land owners including the changing governments. Presently, they also own biggest commercial firms as well as the banks in the country, besides they are co-owners with the government in their various projects. Over the years, they have diversified their economy in textiles/ garment industry as well as in hotel and tourism to have a control on the expanding economic outlets including the consumer retail markets through opening of shopping Malls etc. Their numerical size (nearly 10,000 of them) has not changed since British time. This has been done purposely to retain their superiority because a large number of male members of this group, who could not compete with other ethnic groups or could not be absorbed in sugar estates, were sent to Australia and South Africa to take up the lower grade jobs. However, some of them moved to Australia and other

African nations to occupy managerial positions to help develop the sugar estates. They are mostly concentrated in Curepipe and Floreal where they have their own social and sport clubs. They also own bungalows along the coast and some of them spend the winter months over there. They are still committed to traditions and customary practices of the 19th century. Their women folk are beautiful and are gainfully employed and follow the fashions of Paris. They hardly intermingle with people of other ethnic groups and their children also go to exclusive schools meant for the whites. They do maintain social distance with other ethnic groups and a sort of apartheid does exist in Mauritius as well. The employment to people of their own group is very much linked with the great wealth and kinship links they have with members of their racial group. They marry within their own racial group and despise any African strain in their relationship. Some of them take spouses from families settled in Europe. They have large families because the parents of the spouses also live within the married households. Those of whom, who are not that wealthy live in Victorian houses sheltered by bamboo hedges (Doolooa, 2007)

In 1972 Census, the Chinese numbered 24,084, of whom 11,235 were women (In 1830, they were only 69 Chinese while in 1931 their number had increased to 8,923). By and large, they have been shopkeepers and traders and hardly showed any interest either in agriculture or in sugar plantations. They own large shops in the main towns and as merchants, they are involved in whole sale business. In every corner shop in town and even in the smallest village, they sell a wide range of merchandise and grocery. They are a hardworking group and are also keen to acquire higher education. Some of them have moved into academic and other bureaucratic positions on the island. Those in shopkeeping occupation, some of them, over the years, have become large importers, manufacturers and industrialists. Barring some, by and large, the women have adopted European clothes and way of life. Only one third of them use. Chinese as their day-to-day language while the rest of them speak Creole. The youth who are educated are also employed in most European firms and Banks and the Franco-Mauritians treat them more as equals than the other ethnic groups, despite the fact that they are regarded as a separate distinct group. They are politically shrewd and all major political parties tend to woo them towards their groups by offering them Ministerial births in their respective governments.

The Creoles constitute a very diversified composition, though in 1972 Census, they were clubbed with Franco-Mauritians under the category of general population, yet the term Creole is now applied to a person of European descent but one who is born outside France. In Mauritius, any one who is not of pure French/British, Indian or Chinese blood is labelled as Creole. However, they constitute two groups having separate identities, one of coloured community of mixed European, African/Indian descent and the other of African origin whose descendents gained independence after the abolition of slavery on the island. The origin of coloured persons is linked to the African women slaves whose fathers were European settlers or soldiers, generally of French origin. Later on, the Indian women, to a limited extent, also bore children fathered by Europeans. Numerically, they constituted a substantial group by the time the slavery was abolished but they were never accepted by the Europeans. As such, they maintained their own identity and were mainly French speaking and showed inclination towards Franco-Mauritian's religion, culture and tradition. Like Franco-Mauritians, they too have large family ties. Earlier, they were owning large iron firms but they have no interest in trade and commerce. However, they have been successful in the teaching profession, the civil services, higher clerical jobs and middle level managerial positions in the plantations. But because of easy access to education, some of them also became Barristers and Doctors. They do help people of their group and their relatives to get jobs but they are not economically as affluent as Franco-Mauritians. High level civil servants live in Quatre Bornes while those in junior occupations live in Rose-Hill/Beau Bassin where they have their own clubs. They too have winter bungalows on the sea-side. The other Creoles of African origin are the second largest community in Mauritius. Many of them are skilled artisans and provide much of the labour-force on the island. But they hardly work as agricultural workers, mostly they work as dockers, stevedores and fishermen. Those with education have joined civil service, the police force, and some of them now hold good positions in hotels and private firms owned by the whites. There is no full time employment for all of them and wives of many take up domestic jobs to acquire lodging accommodation. Those engaged in hotel industry and as drivers are fairly well-paid. Their attitude towards life is that of a person who believes in "eat, drink and merry". Because of this, most of them are an impoverished lot and look forward to the state for their poverty alleviation.

Social Stratification: Class and Caste Dimensions

Every society has some form of social stratification. It is based on rank ordering of various categories of individuals or groups, which constitute important units of the community social structure. A number of indicators such as age, sex, physical strength, race or ethnicity, wealth, standard of living and class and community participation have been employed to measure social rank and prestige of an individual. All these characteristics of an individual are highly inter-related and the occupational prestige is considered highly correlated with all of them, because it is a useful indicator of one's family social status and a good indicator of one's children's life chances in the community or society.

We have already discussed the class analysis of ethnic and racial groups in the context of Mauritius in the preceding section. In terms of life-style, standard of living, possession of wealth, we can place Franco-Mauritians or the white settlers at the higher level of Mauritian economy who effectively control it because of the vast amount of wealth with them. Class differences are clearly visible because they are owners of the means of production, have certain political preferences, life style choices, access to better health and educational opportunities and are better placed in terms of levels of income and wealth. Besides them, a small proportion of the Indo-Mauritians (Hindus and Muslims) who have become owners of land and are industrialists and traders constitute the economic elite in the Mauritian society. Further, a small group of Sino-Mauritians who are traders and industrialists also belong to the elite group. It is reported that nearly 3-5 percent of the Mauritian population own nearly three-fourth of the total wealth of the country.

However, due to industrializing and urbanizing influences of a globalized economy and modernization, there is an emergence of middle class in Mauritius mostly constituting the Indo-Mauritians, Sino-Mauritians and Creoles (Nearly 15 to 20 percent). They occupy mostly white collared jobs and have small businesses. They tend to acquire higher consumption pattern and are mostly located in urban pockets. The other better educated among them who have professional qualifications tend to associate themselves in their life-style with the upper class stratum. However, the vast majority of Indo-Mauritians and Creoles belong to the working class in Mauritius and constitute the lower stratum.

They are mostly working as wage labourers either in EPZ firms or in sugar estates and some of them cultivate small plots of land, on a part-time basis. Most of the Creoles in this socio-economic class are fishermen, harbour workers, labourers and factory workers.

As wealth and power appears to be distributed unequally in Mauritius, different social groups have been observed to have conflicting interests because of tough competition between different interest groups. Further, because of having unequal power dimensions, there is a tendency for a group to become dominant over the others. In this way, the dominant group tries to operate the society while keeping its interest above that of the other. As a consequence, the dominant group appropriates a large share of scarce resources such as wealth and enjoys a higher social status. These elites especially those in the political arena have a tendency to take decisions, which benefit them most than those which concern people lower in the social hierarchy. As a result of that, the gap between the rich and the poor increases.

Even in the Mauritian society, certain jobs are considered more valuable than the others and can be analysed within structural-functional perspective of social stratification, since it is argued in this perspective that social stratification is useful for the operation of the society and those who are highly qualified should fill up valuable positions and receive greater rewards than others. The position that an individual holds in Mauritius determines his/her status in the society. Since, social classes are determined according to the degree of prestige that the job gives to an individual, the political elites like Prime Minister, Ministers and Members of Parliament, enjoy a higher social class than the lawyers, judges, doctors and the bureaucrats who constitute the middle class while the labourers and non-literate persons form the lower class.

The entire Mauritian population may be divided into different social classes such as Franco-Mauritians, who may be called the Bourgeoisie of the Mauritian society having higher position, better facilities such as good opportunities for children to go to famous schools and prestigious Universities. The next in order are the Indo-Mauritians who mostly enjoy white-collar jobs having good status. Though, they may enjoy less prestige in occupation than the bourgeoisie class, they are still held in high esteem by the members of the high class. The Sino-Mauritians, mostly traders and businessmen may be like petite bourgeoisie, though some of them enjoy social status equivalent to that of high class. They may enjoy less power, prestige because of their nature of work but in response to globalization processes, some of them have moved into high-end occupations such as tourism, beach resorts and real estate business etc. The last class is that of manual workers who are either planters or factory workers. Because of their nature of job and low salary structure, they are placed at the bottom of the social classes in the contemporary Mauritian Society.

The caste system in Mauritius is reported to be not that rigidly pursued as in India. There are no caste panchayats, which maintain strict discipline among members of their respective caste groups nor are castes related to any specific occupation. However, this institutional structure typical of the Hindu community has been observed to exist in Mauritius among the Indo-Mauritians especially the Hindus who came as indentured labourers or coolies. It is reported, strangely many of them had come to this island country from upper castes of India but the conditions under which they came, lived and worked as labourers make one doubt of their identity of belonging to the upper caste strata. They were supposed to indicate personal description while registering themselves to work on the sugar estates. As the conditions of employment were quite different than what they were in India, it was just possible that many of them who were more intelligent than others and had come from different set of villages without their families from India, might have taken advantage of their immigration circumstances and changed their caste affiliations from lower to that of higher caste in order to seek better employment on the island. Burton, Benedict (1965) who did field work in Mauritius highlighted that there were changes observed in caste status among the Hindus who upgraded them while migrating to the urban areas of the island. They raised their caste status by joining Kshatriya group by adding *singh* to their names and calling themselves as "Babujees". By becoming caste conscious, they joined hands with the so-called Brahmins on the island to monopolise key jobs in the government sector. The people in the lower caste groups who were mostly indentured labourers were the most discriminated ones in seeking employment or promotion in government services. Even their entry to certain government departments was prevented by the high caste Hindus who managed to get scholarships for themselves as well as for their children in foreign universities. However, in the political arena, it is the Vaishya caste group, which has provided Prime Ministerial Leadership (except at one occasion) because of preponderance of their numerical size on the island. The freedom movement had thrown up a number of leaders from the lower caste groups but barring a few, most of them could not make a mark because of the electoral system, developed along caste and ethnic lines. However, the progressive Hindus and the new generation in particular have detested the menace of casteism in modern Mauritius and efforts are being made to decompose the caste structure. One such significant attempt was made by Prime Minister Jugnauth during his tenure to allow persons of castes other than that of Brahmin, Kshatriya group to officiate as priests in the Sanatan Dharma temples and to perform marriage rites in the ceremony. An Ambedkar Memorial Action Research Trust is also emerging as a new institution outfit for safeguarding the legitimate aspirations of the lower caste Hindu groups. (Doolooa, 2007)

Despite the above commendable efforts, by the political system and the non-governmental organizations (NGOs) to dilute the influence of caste system among the Hindus, it is observed that it is still a strong force to reckon with especially in marriage circles and political accomplishments. One of the key informants, who was looking for a suitable match for his Brahmin son was desperate to find one in the same caste group either from the island or from India. He was apprehensive that in case he finds a match for his son from any other group including other upper caste groups, he may have to face the wrath of his close kith and kin on the island. This type of observation also holds good for other caste groups as well, despite a strong Arya Samaj movement on the island, which decries caste system and is a path-breaking venture of Hindu reformed social life. The caste composition also plays a significant role while selecting candidates for Parliamentary as well as Municipal Council and local level elections by political parties of different hues and shades, irrespective of different political ideologies. In fact, the political process evolved on the island as a consequence of coalition politics and power structure has lent support to the resurgence of the caste system among the Hindus. This has also a contagious effect on the Muslim community who also are divided along various sects. It is not in politics alone, but even in marriage circles, the adherences to various sects are given due consideration and weightage. In view of the above, is it possible for Mauritian people to move towards a civil society engineered by a secular character of its population? This is a serious question that needs to be addressed by the economic, social and political elites of the country.

Change in Language Use

Man has evolved a symbol system for his social existence through his interaction with his socio-cultural environment. The programming capability of man gave an edge to him over other species for evolving various complex forms of media of communication for expanding his resources and to have better control of his environments. Language is one such medium evolved by man, out of various symbol systems, to transmit the culture from one generation to another within a group, community or society. Language has evolved its own grammatical connotations to built up knowledge through development of a script. However, communication between human beings has also been made possible through non-evolved scripts, which imply various dialects to interact with one another in a community or society. These are of numerous types and become effective in day to day communication besides contributing to the growth and development of a language instrumental in building knowledge and developing skills among the people (The science of semiotics has three major components, syntactics based on grammatical arrangements of words in speech or writing, semantics referring to meaning in language and pragmatics based on facts related to practical or day to day use of lessons or communication symbols).

In the context of Mauritius, it may be mentioned that in view of multi ethnic composition of the population drawn in from Europe, Africa and Asia, which came over to this island through various waves of immigration, we find different languages in use. However, the most pragmatic way of communication between people on the island is Creole, which is a broken form of French and includes words from other languages such as Hindi, Urdu, Marathi, Tamil, Telugu, Bhojpuri etc. The official language adopted during the British regime as well as after the independence of the country is English. However, the French language continues to dominate as most of the journals and newspapers and periodicals in the island are published in this language.

Over the years, it is observed that there is a change in the use of language mostly spoken at home by the people on this island. As indicated in the **Housing and Population Census, 2000** wherein a comparison has been made in regard to language usually or most spoken at home by the resident population at two points of time, that is, in the year 1990 and 2000. It is observed that though Bhojpuri was spoken by 19.1 percent of the population in 1990, it has gone down to 12.1 percent by 2000. However, for the same period there is an increase of use of Chinese language (from 0.4 to 0.7 percent), Creole (from 61.7 to 71.1 percent), English (from 0.2 to 0.3 percent), French (from 3.3 to 3.4 percent) and others (combination of languages from 1.5 to 12 percent). On the other hand, there is a decline in the use of Hindi from 1.2 to 0.6 percent, Marathi from 0.7 to 0.2 percent, Tamil from 0.8 to 0.3 percent, Telugu from 0.6 to 0.2 percent and Urdu from 0.6 to 0.1 percent, for the same period, that is over the decade of 1990 to 2000.

It is disheartening to note, as indicated by the above data, that there has been a steady decline in the use of Indian languages including Urdu over the years and may be by the next Census, these may show further decline in their use by the inhabitants at home. Though, there is a slight increase in the use of English and French at home by the resident population while speaking to each other, yet the overwhelming increase of nearly ten percent over the decade of the use of Creole only sends disturbing signals to the cultural identity of different ethnic groups. There is danger of "Creolization" of the population, in terms of cultural conquest of a particular dialect over the well-developed languages including English, French, Hindi and Urdu. The vehicle of communication which builds up the cultural core value system of any ethnic group gets threatened and despite efforts made by the state to promote Indian Languages in schools, colleges as well as by the Mahatma Gandhi Institute (MGI), the cultural onslaught of Creole which does not have script of its own may cause disequilibrium in the cultural and social life of people. Even the efforts made by English and French schools to promote their respective languages seem to be falling prey to the increasing use of Creole on the island.

Creolization may not be conceived only in terms of communication or linguistic use but even it might affect the life style of people and there may be tendency on the part of individuals or groups to imbibe values of a particular ethnic group which is weak in work ethics and prove counter productive to the development process. Some linguists have been making efforts to develop a script for the Creole dialect but they have failed to evolve it. Others are of the view that use of Creole binds the people of different ethnic or cultural groups and may be an asset to the unity of the Republic of Mauritius. As such, the linguistic policy on the island should be kept open and flexible so as to maintain the concept of unity in diversity.

Despite the lingua-franca of all Mauritians being Creole, some persons in the middle classes are also fluent in English and French. Gujaratis seem to be sticking to the use of their mother tongue at home whereas Calcuttya Muslims like their other North Indian Hindu immigrants speak Bhojpuri but it is a dying language, spoken only by the older generation. Urdu is commonly used in mosques and most of the Muslims identify it as an Arabic language. Apart from promoting languages of Asian origin for example Mandarin for the Chinese, Urdu, Hindi, Tamil, Telugu and Marathi for Indo-Mauritians in schools, there is an air time provided by the electronic media to encourage development of these languages.

The interesting observation made is that in all religious congregations to celebrate various fairs and festivals of different ethnic groups (Hindus, Muslims, Christians etc) though, initially the organizers of such functions may start their speeches in the respective languages of different communities but soon they switch over to the use of Creole as a medium of communication. Often on television, it is observed that the newscasters are well-decked in Indian sarees or sub-continent dresses and they look very ethnic in their presentation but their communication in Creole makes one feel the over-whelming acculturating influence of one dominant culture over the other. One gets a feeling that often there is a kind of cultural split, which may result in developing ambivalent attitudes among individuals who want to modernize but yet retain their traditional frailings. It may be that in due course of time, the globalising influences through modernisation syndrome may transform the personality structure of individuals and groups who may become more rational and practical in their behaviour pattern.

Changes in Family, Marriage and Gender Status

Family, marriage and status of women are highly interrelated. Family as an institution is universal in its existence. Every society has some form of family institution existing as the socialization of children is basically done through it. The transmission of culture to the children and the psycho-social protection to them, the emotional and sentimental support, division of labour for pursuing economic activities among the members, "we" feeling among members based on consanguinal or blood ties, has reckoned family a socio-psychic, cultural and economic necessity. Further, the affinal kinship relationships which are acquired through marriage extend the span of family circle. It is observed that in the patriarchal societies of Asia and Africa, the family residential pattern is mostly patrilocal while the family structure has been observed to be joint. This holds good particularly for Indian communities who have even migrated across the other parts of the world. The individuals when they move out of the joint family structure to constitute nuclear units, still maintain links and ties with the core family unit and in times of absolute necessity of help and crisis, they look towards it for support. However, as a consequence of modernizing influences due to industrialization and urbanization, there is an increasing trend towards nuclearlization of the family. Yet, it is observed that the extended ties with the joint family set-up are maintained for all practical purposes. In the context of Mauritius, it has been observed that now there is an increasing trend towards the formation of nuclear family units but the base of family structure is still extended or joint in nature especially among the Indo-Mauritians and people of Chinese origin. The main reasons for a shift in family structure are marital independence, better educational and employment opportunities, internal migrations due to employment facilities, better economic status, and independence in beliefs and value patterns, as a consequence of modernising influences. People belonging to the younger age group are opting to acquire a nuclear family structure after marriage. There is also a tendency now to have small family size and this change at the attitude level is an indication of the negative consequences of a large family structure. In times of need, stress or help, however, they do look towards their extended family units and expect co-operation from their close kith and kin, especially their own relatives, wive's relatives and friends. Of course, there is also more leaning shown towards the brides' parents and relatives' side than bridegroom's parents side to avoid any intra familiar conflict between the mother-in-law and daughter-in-law (Mehta, 1981).

However, with increasing employment opportunities to women in industry, commercial establishments and government sector, the nuclear family units are finding it hard to integrate themselves as harmonious groups because of both husbands and wives, taking up employment. This has now caused a strain in maintaining marital relationships and as a consequence of that, there is a higher risk of breakdown of marriage and consequently the family as an institution has now become highly vulnerable. No doubt, families have always been subjected to change when children are born or when they marry and leave their families or while they are adult and take up employment, even as a result of death of one's spouse or in the event of divorce etc. Though, the "positional family" is more stable but it is less favoured by the young who prefer to be child free. At times, women want full time work and prefer personal marriage, yet in recent times, there is emergence of marriages between people of the same sex, which are very rare and are looked down upon in Mauritius. Like most western countries, statistically speaking, more families in Mauritius are nuclear and even the divorce rate is increasing. Yet it has been observed that from these families, in a number of cases, the children are left to the care of their grand parents when both parents are at work. Despite being nuclear units, quite often, the spouses may take meals at the home of their parents. Some couples may prefer to continue staying with their parents not because of any emotional or traditional ties but to save money to buy their own home or in certain cases they may construct accommodation for living above the parents' house or adjoining to their residences. In such cases, major decisions are likely to be taken by the couple with the support of the extended family and not by the elder member of the family.

It is apparent from the study done on the evolution of women in Mauritius (Mauritius Research Council) that a clear-cut categorization cannot be made of Mauritian families. In some aspects, the family is traditional while in others, it is based on personal relationships and is unconventional. The traditional family structure is changing to accommodate the need for generating higher incomes in order to aspire for better socio-economic status in the society. As such, whether a family acquires traditional structure or moves on to a nuclear pattern would depend upon economic as well as the other socio-cultural factors (Hawoldar, Ragobur et al, 2004).

Closely related to family is the institution of marriage. In fact, both are complementary to each other. Although, there have been different forms of marriages observed in various societies, yet in the modern era, the monogamous form of marriage for contracting marital relationships got evolved. Historically speaking, this pattern got evolved from the promiscuous, group and polygamous form of marriages, practiced among persons of opposite sex in different cultural and civilizational levels. However, the normative aspects of marriage make it sacrosanct and any deviation from it causes disequilibrium in the family structure.

In the context of Mauritius and other outer islands of Mauritius, historically it is observed that slaves were mainly brought from Mozambique as well as from Madagascar and the groups, which inhabited them, developed a peculiar matriarchal family structure. Early sexual intercourse, weak couple or marital links as well as astute ways of sharing fluid company became the norm. The off springs of such unions were often taken care of by the mothers. The mother was in any case the single parent recognized under slavery till the amelioration laws of 1829 and this pattern continued later on. The typical marital tradition that got evolved in the islands followed a pattern, as given next. At 15-16 years of age, a young man left his mother's hut and with the help of his friend constructed his own hut and furnished it. A young girl left her family's hut at around 14-15 years with her "trousseau" and went to live as "concubinage" with the boy. If marriage was considered between the two, the young man's parents made a formal proposal to the girl's parents. With their consent, the manager of the estate conducted the ceremony in the presence of the priest. But in certain cases, the couple chose to wait till the next visit of the priest to the island. Each women accepted one or more partners besides her acknowledged one who visited in turn at night and had to leave before the day break. They were known as "Noirs Bonsoirs" and had to contribute some labour or tasks for the family (Chajoo and Bablee, 2007).

Even, in Rodrigues, which is a part of Republic of Mauritius, formal marriage is not common among men and women and they live together which is considered a very normal practice. Migrants from this island to Mauritius living in Bambous also continue following the same practice. The cut term coined for this practice among the youth is "take away". This practice which is a part of Rodrigues culture is also observed in Mauritius. Males attach much importance to having children whereas the women do not show any kind of specific interest (Din Dayal, 2007).

However, over the years with the development of the Mauritian island, people prefer to have spouses who are educated, have good temperament and are of good health, are religious, have a good reputation, enjoy economic standing and have good physical appearance. Further, people would prefer that the boys are married around 24 years and girls around 19 years of age. However, in the villages people would prefer that their girls are married off below the age of 19 years, as there is a tendency for the girls to drop out from the schools after primary level. Besides, there is a moral dimension also attached for an early marriage of girls in the rural areas. But with the increase of employment opportunities for girls and with the secondary education made free, the marriage age of girls has risen beyond 19 years of age. As regards, inter-community or inter-religious marriages, though these are preferred by the educated and well placed individuals or groups on the island, yet these are solemnized only on a limited scale. By and large, these are contracted within the same religious, ethnic or caste groups especially among the Hindus. It is felt by the parents that inter-community or inter-caste marriages involve problems related to adaptation of different social and cultural values and many of them fear from being ex-communicated from the community or religious institutions. A few cases that have been observed on the island related to inter community or caste marriages appear to be a class phenomenon. Though, people prefer religious marriages, yet officially these are considered invalid for the inheritance of the property after the death of the spouse. As such, they are required to get their marriages registered at the Civil Status Office. But invariably, people ignore it and this gives rise to extra-marital relations and polygamous marriages, resulting in the increase of delinquent children thereby rendering the institution of family very weak. (Mehta, 1981).

A recent survey sponsored by Mauritius Research Council to study the evolution of gender and development in Mauritius (carried out in 1998-2000 by Prof. Martha

Fowlkes) has thrown some interesting findings in regard to marriage and status of women. It is reported that now marriage is not considered to be the only destiny for women. There is a change observed in the thinking and attitudes among the people as economic self-reliance in girls is considered to be important before they get married. It is also acknowledged now that education of girls has enhanced their chances of a better marriage and younger women showed aversion for financial dependency either on husbands or fathers. However, this was not the case with the middle aged and older women. It was also observed that 39.3 percent of the respondents mentioned that they chose their own marriage partners against 37.7 percent who had an arranged marriage. This is indicative of the fact that women are increasingly having a greater say in marriage. (Hawoldar, Ragobur et al, 2004).

It may be pertinent to mention here that currently marriage is no longer being viewed as an institution for procreation and providing life-long stability for women. The urban educated girls prefer to postpone their marriage to satisfy their career ambitions as they feel that they should stand on their feet first and marriage can come later on. In fact, there is an intergenerational gap and the girls today are different than those of their mothers' generation and they want an equal relationship in marriage. Of course, this has resulted in making marriages fragile leading to a higher incidence of their breakdown. As a consequence of that, the divorce rate has been on the rise and the institution of family in the Mauritian society is becoming highly vulnerable to change.

Closely related to the institutions of family and marriage is the status of women. In patriarchal societies, women have always played a second fiddle to their male counterparts. It is the husband who has always influenced the decisions in the family and played an active role as a chief familial actor in maintaining inter-family relationships within as well as outside the community. However, as a consequence of better educational and employment opportunities, mass media exposure, urbanizing and industrialising influences, the right to vote and the will to assert equity with men, women, by and large, have assumed a modern outlook and are now making a clarion call for improving their status. There is now a tendency to favour education of girls and it was observed that in the context of Mauritius, more number of girls than boys are not only going in for secondary and higher education, but also excelling in different streams in these examinations. No doubt, there is still a greater preference for the sons over daughters to go in for secondary and university education but now there is a shift in the attitude of the people and they are favouring the education of their daughters. Even there are a large number of persons in the rural areas who because of the education of their daughters are favourably disposed towards the employment of girls. As a result of setting up of export free-zone industries, manufacturing and garment industries, tourism promoting beach hotels and resorts, call centres due to opening up of IT sector, expansion of education and health services on the island, increase of banking and financial institutions, women are increasingly seeking employment to enhance their social status.

Further, it was observed that because of enhanced status of women, they are now consulted by men on matters related to family affairs, practically on all matters and to a limited extent on some matters.

Women have got awareness regarding their rights and they now expect equitable behaviour for them on family matters especially related to choosing marriage partner establishing nuclear family units to avoid intra-familial disputes and activities related to religious ceremonies. However, in the rural areas, still a large proportion of families would like to find out a prospective opportunity for marriage of their daughters rather than encouraging them to go in for higher education or find suitable employment. In both, agricultural and industrial sectors, women are paid less wages than their male counterparts. This kind of discrimination on gender basis lowers their status in the community. The state must ensure that as a part of human rights, they should be provided with certain integrative, legal or social measures, to provide equitable justice to them to avoid any kind of social disturbance (Mehta,1981). Again the study on evolution of gender and development in Mauritius carried out for the Mauritius Research Council (by Prof. Martha Fowlkes (1998-2000)) has brought out that as a result of indirect and direct developmental inputs, there has been an improvement in the conditions, status and relations between men and women. Further, equal access to education has been provided and it has been recognized that education is equally important for boys and girls. In certain quarters, it is felt that education is even more important for girls. It is also observed that there is an improvement in the socialization of women both at homes and schools and they have moved out of the behaviour of docility and submissiveness to that of assertiveness and confidence. This type of behaviour is not cherished by older men and women especially those in the villages. However, gender bias in favour of boys with respect to investment in higher education has declined as nearly three fourth of the respondents did not agree that higher education was more important for boys than for girls. More men than women supported this proposition. Further, a large proportion of respondents believed that girls and boys were equally intelligent but nearly three-fourth of them also indicated that men were by nature superior to women, thus supporting the macho image of man. The terms like gender and feminism were not understood by a majority of the population. The majority of respondents attributed improvement in the status of women to education, legal reforms and economic empowerment, which has given them self-confidence. However, it is also believed that economic empowerment has made women more arrogant and this is not viewed as a positive indicator of development. The patriarchal control of men over women in the family, no doubt, is on the decline, yet there is a belief in certain quarters that women should stay at home and care for home and children and if economic necessity compels them to move out for work, only then they should seek employment. A higher proportion of respondents are of the view (67 percent) that men should be given preference over women in recruitment, as men are believed to be superior. This only shows that gender equality in employment is contested and not supported fully.

No doubt, nearly three fourth of the respondents believe that women can provide good leadership as equal to that of men and more women should be inducted into the position of leadership but this proposition seems to be supported more by women than men. Nearly half of the respondents also believe that women are not decisive enough to become good leaders. This may explain the glass-ceiling situation. Nearly all the respondents (94.5 percent) believed that alcoholism was a major social problem affecting adversely the quality of life of people and it is also reported by the majority of respondents that women should not drink any alcohol. Almost, all respondents (95 percent) favoured that husbands should share responsibility for cooking, cleaning and child care. Moreover, nearly half of them thought that arranged marriages worked better than love marriages. However, cultural differences were observed to be significant in this regard. As regards the issue of abortion, the respondents were more or less equally divided. But, the sexist attitude was weakening. Further, the role of men was reported to be significant in maintaining family and shouldering their responsibilities towards it. Slightly more than half of the respondents believed that there was more of physical violence in society, in as much as 15.4 percent were accepting verbal violence between spouses and 9 percent were accepting physical violence.

In the final analysis, it is pointed out that Mauritian women have been subjected to social, legal and administrative changes which provided them opportunities to achieve in their personal and professional lives. However, they have yet to face a number of challenges to ease out their frustrations and make full use of legal and other provisions available to them to enhance capacity building, management skills, upgrading skills in use of technology at all levels to provide creative leadership and build up women entrepreneurs, decision makers, political leaders, in different strata of the Mauritian society (Hawoldar, Ragobur, et. al 2004).

However, the serial marriages, live-in relationships, desertion of wives by husbands in certain cases, children born out of wedlock due to live-in relationships may be responsible for lowering the status of women in the Mauritian society. Instead of clamouring for feminism and masculinity, there is a need to enhance effective communication and interaction between spouses /persons of both sexes to avoid gender conflicts and blaming each other for his or her role to develop a harmonious society.

Religion and Secularism

The English word “Religion” has its roots in Latin word “Religare” which means binding together or the concept of a group or fellowship. It may suggest exclusion of individuals but an individual as a member of the group, has personal beliefs, emotions and thoughts and can associate him or herself to any religious system. But religion as a group phenomenon is manifested by religious congregation, ceremonial gatherings, denominations, prayer meetings and family pilgrimages. Religion may be defined as a system of beliefs and practices of a group of people who interpret and respond to what they feel as sacred and usually as a supernatural power which is not subject to the laws of the observable universe, for example, such a power may be personified by Jesus, Vishnu, Allah or by any number of Gods, Devils, Goblins, Spirits etc. On the other hand, secularism has been coined in 1851 by George Jacob Holyrake as a rationalist movement of protest in England and it was then built into the ideology of progress. It is considered as a process of modernity by some scholars and it provides enlargement of human freedom, besides the enhancement of the range of choices open to people for things that concern them most, including their present and future life-style. Secularism is also considered by some as a process by which sectors of society and culture are removed from the domination of religious institutions and symbols. In short, what was considered religious earlier ceases to be so because of the processes of differentiation making economic, political, legal and moral dimensions discrete from each other based on the dimension of rationality which replaces traditional beliefs and ideas by modern knowledge (Johnstone, 1988).

In the context of Mauritius as mentioned earlier, there are three major religious groups such as Christianity, Islam and Hinduism, besides a small section of Chinese who practiced Buddhism. People belonging to Islam and Hinduism are divided into a number of sects which follow different customs and rituals. The Christians in majority belong to

Roman Catholic faith and the first church was built in Port Louis in 1737 which allowed the flow of priests and missionaries to the island and spread of Roman Catholic faith. This was also embraced by some Chinese and Muslims. All Christian festivals are celebrated and those in urban areas attend the services regularly and more frequently than those in the non-urban areas. The Anglican Church is small and attended mainly by British whites who have a limited population now in the island. Besides, it is also frequented by small members of Indian and Creole communities. The Islamic religion of the Muslims is more highly organized than that of the Hindu faith. The nature of Islam itself is based on the tenets laid for Muslim community and it has held this minority group together while the early wealthy Muslim merchants have consolidated it by supporting their religion financially. There are over 65 mosques in Mauritius while the main Muslim mosque is located in Port Louis (Jumma Mosque). Each mosque is managed by Mutwali who is elected by congregation. All the mosques practically have been constituted as *waqfs* administered by *waqf* boards set up by government ordinance of 1941 (The main function is to make permanent decision related to Muslim property including building and income for religious or charitable purposes as defined by the laws of Islam). A mosque is a focal point of the Muslim community and around it the *jammat* or religious and social activities take place. The majority of Muslims belong to the orthodox group of Sunnis. However, a small group of Shias who follow a different Islamic tradition also considers themselves as orthodox. A small group of Ahmediyas (sect founded in the Panjab in the undivided India by Mirja Ghulam Ahmed who claimed to be the Messiah of Muslims) considers this sect similar to the reform group of the Hindus. There appears intense social interaction among various Muslim groups and they tend to preserve individual identities in both the rural and urban areas, The Muharram, Yauji-in-Naki, Eid-ul-Fitr and Eid-ud-Azha are the main Muslim festivals celebrated in Mauritius.

The Hindu faith is the most popular on the island because of numerical dominance of the community on the island. The Hindus do not have any organized church but they are having a number of associations operating at the national and local levels. The Roman Catholic church was subsidized from 1790 onwards but the Hindu religious organizations got subsidies from the government for the practicing of their religion after a long "Jan Andolan Movement" initiated by Basdeo Bissoondoyal Brothers. However, it was Basdeo Bissoondoyal who established a solid base to the Hindu religion by bringing together the two important sects of Hindus, that is, the Sanatanists and Arya Samajists. He was also responsible for awakening the Hindus and making efforts towards the Independence of the country by launching his political outfit 'Indian Forward Block' (IFB). Hindu ceremonies are organized both in temples and private homes by a Brahmin or a Pandit who officiates at various gatherings and opens the meetings with a prayer. In almost all houses in the villages as well as in towns, there is a fluttering Red flag and a small idol of a Hindu God or Goddess (mainly Hanumanji) in the front yard. This indicates that the house belongs to a Hindu inhabitant.

In the beginning of 20th century there was birth of Arya Samaj movement on the Island, which was a reformist move to segregate people from the orthodox Hinduism of Sanatan Dharma. This was initiated by Mani Lal Doctor, an emissary of Mahatma Gandhi, who visited the island for a short period and made a clarion call for the dissolution of caste system, discarding of purdah system, education of girls, discarding of orthodox rights and the belief that only Brahmins can perform religious ceremonies. No doubt, the orthodox Hindus belonging to the Sanatan Dharma, reacted vehemently against the Arya Samaj movement which was promoting setting up of Hindi schools and teaching of Hindi in them all over the island as well as encouraging the non-brahmins to perform orthodox ceremonies. There are more than 100 temples which are managed by two religious federations or associations of the Sanatan Dharma whereas there are more than 400 Arya Sabhas across the island with their headquarter in the Port Louis. Unfortunately, there are factious groups observed both in the Sanatan Dharma and Arya Samaj sects practiced by the Hindus. The two Sanatan federations or associations are managing nearly an equal number of temples on the island while the Arya Samaj has Arya Ravived and the Arya Pratinidhi Sabhas. Despite efforts made to bring the factions of both the sects together, it has not been possible to do so but there appears now a better understanding and co-operation between the various factions through the efforts of the political and social elites. Ramayana epic is very popular in the rural areas and its reading in vernacular is held in towns whereas in the rural areas it is disseminated to the people through Baithikas, now replaced by a common meeting place where religious rites and special ceremonies are performed by a Pandit or a member of the group. The most prominent Hindu festivals are Diwali, Holi and Sankranti. Religious rituals have been observed to be sacrosanct for "Ganga Snan" during Mahashivratri, besides, in fire walking and cavadee festivals of the Tamil Hindus. Mahashivratri festival of the Hindus is observed to be of the longest duration on the island, lasting for nearly 5 days. All young and old men and women and children in their special dress of white colour or sarees (worn by women folk), walk from across the different regions of the island while carrying specially designed "Cavadees" to the Ganga Talab (it has the same religious sanctity as Ganges in India) and after taking "snan" and doing rituals, people, in groups, get back to the respective temples of their area and perform Shivratri puja. Enroute to Ganga Talab, there are "pandals" established all along the roads leading to this place from various directions of the island and the pilgrims are provided shelter in the Pandals. They are allowed to stay in them for the night, if necessary and are given food and 'Parshad' etc. This festival integrates the people of Hindu faith of all shades and hives (Doolooa, 2007).

On the dimension of religion, Mauritius can be called a "Community of Communities", since it appears to have a deep influence on the way of life of the people. No doubt, people of different communities, adhere strictly to their religious beliefs, yet there is a mutual sharing of festivities also. There is a strange admixture of faith and recreation observed, in the sense that older people show lot of reverence for the various deities and perform rituals and rites with sanctity while the younger persons are mostly inclined towards the recreational aspects of the festivals. It has been observed that apart from celebration of festivals at the individual or group level, there appears bureaucratisation of these festivals as a number of religious organizations both among the Hindus and the Muslims are celebrating them on a larger scale for wider participation. This bureaucratisation has resulted into emergence of pressure groups within different communities, which acquire an authority pattern and get political patronage. This has diluted the significance of the sanctity of each religious group on the island. The fact that no body wants to drop any of the festivals, is indicative of the importance of festivities in their life as they believe that they can get an opportunity to get together, share their values, inculcate faith in different beliefs and avail of tension releasing mechanisms for a happy living.

The attendance at religious institutions whether a church, mosque or a temple by a large number of people of respective groups show that religion plays an important part in their day to day life. They want to maintain their religious identity for fear of cultural massagination or because of fear of natural hazards such as cyclone etc. to which they are subjected from time to time. The mistrust which gets built up between different religious groups retards the secularisation process which is an important requisite for the modernization of the people on this island, being governed by parliamentary system of democracy. A large majority of the people worship deities of their respective religious groups and in regard to rationalization of attitudes for worshipping deities in the event of illness in the family or any other crises, not only persons of the Hindu faith but also those of Christian or Muslim faith, worship them to get relief. The most significant observation is in regard to the festival of "Cavadee" where even young boys and girls are subjected to pricking of needles for the fulfilment of certain of their desires including recovery from illness (Mehta, 1981).

Mauritius, though, has adopted democratic governance as a part of its state management yet in reality the structurization of religion because of the multiplicity of sects within each religious group builds up water tight compartments and a hierarchical order is maintained even for contracting marriages between different sects. This formalization of religion makes the society non-secular in character though the state in its constitutional commitment declares it as secular. It has been observed that practically in all religious festivities or functions, the political elites make use of the platforms provided to them to woo voters for their political ends, in anticipation of the elections. However, if we conceive secularisation in the context of Gandhian perspective of tolerance of one religious group towards the other, and not conceiving it in terms of beyond religious dogmas towards people of different religious adherences, then, perhaps, Mauritius may be rightly called as a society moving towards secularisation. To build up a secular character of the nation, it is desirable that religion should be pursued at the personal level or in the private sphere and it should be discouraged in the public sphere. Its pronouncement in the public sphere politicises it and makes it more traditional in its influence on the masses, thereby retarding the development process.

Globalizing Social and Cultural Life

Globalisation has been conceived mainly in terms of homogenizaton of the developing nations by the developed nations by integrating them economically through complex economic connections, stretching across the world. The products which have been manufactured across hundred different countries are regularly transported over the globe. These social, political and economic connections have crossed borders between countries and have affected the lifestyle of the people living in them. In fact, globalisation, through flow of information, has resulted in increasing interdependence of the world society (Giddens, 1989)

However, for the developing nations, globalisation processes have resulted in having not only economic but also political hegemony of the developed nations over them, besides the onslaught of cultural invasions of the modern western nations on the life-style of the people residing in them. In the context of Mauritius, which is an isolated nation cut off from the rest of the world and connected only through air and sea, the globalizing influences mostly have come through neighbouring areas especially South Africa. Britain and France which had colonial hold on the Island for centuries and also brought in the modernization of the Island in terms of establishing infra structural facilities like power, shipments, airways, roads, telecommunications, sugar, tea and tobacco plantations as well as their milling operations, water sprinkling irrigation facilities, education and health care facilities. These changed the social and cultural life of the people on the island especially those inhabiting the urban areas. After sugar boom on the island, there was a construction boom and as a result of that people started replacing their tin or asbestos houses by building up concrete houses. Now, in the rural areas, one hardly comes across the traditional house structures except in some of the coastal villages. People are conscious of improving their living conditions by having better housing, internal access roads, social welfare centres, health centres, tapped water, play grounds, children parks, TV antennas, music systems, modern electronic gadgets and cooking appliances etc. Even with a network of well set roads, flyovers, expressways, there has been rise in the different means of transport communication such as imported cars of all brands from across the auto-world, motorcycles, buses, scooters etc. Moreover, over the years, there is a considerable improvement in the traffic inflow and outflow of people from the rural to urban centres. The emergence of middle class on the island has resulted in making use of these facilities. Further, though, electrification of the entire island has been taken care of, yet water supply is a problem in certain areas and it depends on the quantum of rainfall in a season to fill up the water reservoirs to their full capacity. Even in village localities, gadgets like radio cassettes, television sets, electric rice cookers and refrigerators are considered prized possessions to raise their social status in the community.

Globalizing influences have been marked more in urban centres and towns than in rural areas. There is a tremendous change in the food habits and dress patterns of the people. Traditional dress like Dhoti, Kurta in the case of male and saree in the case of female is getting replaced by T-shirts, trousers, jeans, frocks, tops, skirts etc. There is now an increasing number of shopping malls, complexes and shopping centres that have come up in the main cities as well as in the nearby towns where products, wares and artefacts are brought from South Africa, France, Britain, India, Pakistan, and China for the consumption not only of the urban elites but also for the rural inhabitants. Besides, increased shopping facilities, there is opening of restaurants, hotels, eatries like Kentucky Fried Chicken (KFC), Pizza Hut, Dominos managed and run by MNCs, bars, casinos, discos, pubs, and open restaurants especially at Caudan Water Front at the Port Louis harbour which is believed to have been shaped on the pattern of Cape Town (South Africa). The younger generation of both boys and girls are the frequent visitors to these places. Their life-style, mannerism and behaviour pattern appears to have changed considerably and they tend to acquire more of European life-style as well as values and feel pride in having these on the island to lead a modern social life.

In addition to above, there are cinema houses, which have become now better designed, and they show Indian, French and English movies. The high end technologies like Information and Communication Technology (ICT) and the promotion of tourism on the island through establishment of Beach hotels, resorts and restaurants apart from providing employment opportunities to the young boys and girls, have also altered the social relationships between different groups and there appears an acquiring of personalized character and formal disposition of behaviour patterns as witnessed in the developed western nations. Apart from the football culture developed in the island by the youth club organizations as a sporting activity, music and dance is an essential part of the Mauritian cultural life. The prominent dance form is "Sega dance", a heritage of African-Creoles which they brought from that subcontinent and people of all ethnic groups dance to the beats of drum and its orchestra. Indian classical dances are also getting popular among the Indo-Mauritians especially through the efforts of the Mahatma Gandhi Institute. The Indian music based on the Hindi movies is the most popular one and every car owner or taxi driver would tune on the cassette or radio to hear it and appreciate the musical composition of songs, even if many of them may not be understanding their meanings as most of them communicate in Creole language. Television as a medium of communication has made efforts to project programmes based on religious faith of different ethnic groups, soaps, serials, and fairs and festivals of Chinese, Christians, Muslims and that of Hindus. To cap these all, in addition to illuminations done on Diwali celebrations and Chinese New year, the Christmas and New Year celebrations are done with great pomp and show where parties and dances become a part of musical bonanza.

The above modernizing influences, no doubt, have brought a change in the social and cultural life of the people and they tend to become modern, yet in most of the cases because of family compulsions, the youth find it hard to shed off the traditional way of life. In fact, there is a paradox of modern co-existing with traditional social life on the island. In the transitional phase, people are moving from inner directed to outer directed modern orientations. This shift in social outlook and lifestyle may get transformed over the years due to increasing globalizing influences of modernization and the island nation may move from community to societal formation.

References

Burton, Benedict (1965) *Indians in a Plural Society*, London, Her Majesty Service

Chajoo, Amenah Jahangear and Bablee, Dianna (2007), "Outer Islands of Mauritius: Historical Overview" *Journal of Mauritian Studies*, New Series, Vol. 3. No. 2, pp. 2-43.

Dindayal, Jutin, (2007), "Sociological study of Rodriguon Community in Mauritius" *Journal of Mauritian Studies* (New Series), Vol. 3. No. 2 pp. 94-103.

Doolooa, Atma (2007) *Castes in Mauritius: The Future of Indians and Hinduism*, New Delhi, Star Publications Pvt. Ltd. (Published Mahrain Ltd. STE, Anne Street, Central Flag, Mauritius).

Giddens, Anthony (1989), *Sociology*. Cambridge, Polity Press.

Hawoldar, Shakuntala, Ragobur Satinder et. al. (2004), *So that Flowers may Bloom: A brief History of the Intergenerational struggle towards Women's Empowerment in Mauritius*, United Nations Development Programme, Mauritius.

Hammel, E.A., (1990), "A Theory of Culture for Demography" *Population and Development Review*, Vol 16. No.3.

Johnstone, Ronald, L (1988). *Religion in Society: Sociology of Religion* (Third Edition) New Jersey, Prentice hall, Englewood Cliffs.

Mehta, S.R. (1981) *Social Development in Mauritius: A study on Rural Modernization in an Island Community*, New Delhi, Wiley Eastern Limited.

Mehta S.R. (1999), *Dynamics of Development: A Sociological Perspective*, New Delhi, Gyan Publishing House.

Peterson, R.A. (1976), "The Production of Culture" *American Behavioural Scientist* Vol. 19. pp. 669-684.

6

Social Transformation of an Island Nation: Development Wonder in Mauritius

Social Transformation

Change is the law of nature. There is a kind of metamorphosis going on among infra as well as human species. The change in human beings may be observed in the form, outward appearance, character and dispositions. This change may be induced or based on natural development of human beings who constitute a group, community or society.

Human nature is based on certain assumptions. First, human being is a biological organisation having physiological drives, needs, potentials and limitations. Secondly, human beings have a programming capability and ability to use symbols. In other words, they can attach meanings to things, sounds, words, acts enacted by them and arrive at consensus on the same to communicate and accumulate knowledge and share it within a group. The language, thus, evolved becomes the prime symbolic mechanism to express ideas with abstract concepts and emotions. Thirdly, people become human only in groups. To substantiate it, the role of socialization of human organism is significant in transmission of information or knowledge to the group or community members. Fourthly, human action is in some form and to certain degree a problem solving act or mechanism. Finally, all social phenomena within a given social group, community or society are integrated (Johnstone, 1988).

Based on the above premises, often the term social transformation has been interchangeably used with that of social change. The other cognate terms employed in sociological discipline for social change, have been evolution, advancement, progress, revolution and development. These have distinct meanings, connotations and applications for analysing and understanding human relations. It is observed that the anthropological Man became social first before he or she entered into economic relations and acquired an authority pattern to become a political Man. It is in the above sense, it is argued that all economic and political phenomena are social in nature and together these constitute the total reality of human life. In the social space, human beings have entered into social relations that acquire endurability and stability over time and to realize their survival, affiliation and psychic needs, they have evolved institutions, which regulate their relationships and become operative in their actions to achieve them. In the process, the norms and values developed to regulate or operate these institutions become the guiding principles in day-to-day life of the people. The core value system evolved within institutions signifies the identity of the human groups, interacting and interrelating with one another, while maintaining their identities but influencing mutually to effect changes within or between groups, or within a community or society. When we define transformation, it means in literal sense, a change from one form to another. However, in the context of social transformation, it implies a kind of either structural or functional change in social relations, institutions, values and identities embodying human life.

In sociology, both evolutionary and revolutionary perspectives have been in vogue to explain the phenomenon of social change. However, both of these are mediated in the conception of development, which has now become an all encompassing concept denoting economic growth as well as social and cultural change. Often, the sociological analysis focuses either on individuals or societies but at the meso level, the community which acts as an intermediary between the micro (individual) or macro (societal) levels, gets ignored. This needs to be examined for showing better understanding of the social transformation of people.

In the context of Mauritius, apart from analysing changes at the individual level in terms of rational orientation and modern outlook, the focus has to be in understanding the changes observed in social relations, institutions, identities and values while the nation-state moves from community to its societal formation in response to the development initiatives over the last four decades or so. In the shift from community (Gemeinschaft) to society (Gesellschaft), the transformative changes in social relationships may be expected to move from informal ties based on primordial dimensions such as age, sex, religion, ethnicity, language etc in community setting to formal ties based on individualistic tendencies, personalized orientations, rational rather than affective outlook etc in the evolvement of society. Even the institutional changes observed from movement of community to society setting will be marked by emergence of modern political and legal structures, new economic institutions like banking, trading, international trading including offshore banking and financial institutions, high end technological institutions like information technology, outsourcing of information through call centres, engineering and medical technology which are a departure from the traditional institutions of colonial regimes such as feudal lord-labour relation organizations, money-lending devices, trading contracts, petty business organizations besides inadequate educational and health care services. These transformative changes, being structural in nature, are not reversible.

However, in the context of social transformation of human group identities and the core values of the institutional webs evolved or created by them, the changes effected within the different groups being adaptive rather than radical, because of democratic governance pursued by the island nation, have been observed to be considerable but these institutions are still intact to a great extent. This is indicative of the fact that the changes in the social structure and value system of the people lag behind the fast economic and political changes triggered off by the development processes. As a consequence of this cultural lag phenomenon, the development of the nation is not inclusive but it is observed to be uneven and socially exclusive.

Development Wonder of an Island Nation

In the context of developing nations, development has to be "people" centric to make it inclusive through providing everyone with ever increasing opportunities for a better life. This may warrant an equitable distribution of income and other social resources to promote social justice, efficient production, raising employment opportunities, expansion and improvement in education, health, nutritional facilities and social and cultural well being of people. The qualitative and structural changes need to go in unison with economic progress while the racial, ethnic and social inequalities must be substantially brought down. It has now been well recognized that development has not to be measured in terms of growth only but to be explicitly expressed as growth and social change. In the new conception of development, it has to be viewed as an overall process of transforming men and societies to a new social order for providing every human being with moral and material well being. In fact, development has to be considered as an integral whole cultural process, which should encompass the natural environment, social relations, education, production, consumption and well being of people. (Dag Hammarskjold Report on Development and International Cooperation, 1975, Mehta, 1984).

In the above context, development interventions by the state should focus on "growth plus social change" as its main goal. In other words, accelerated economic growth and structural change should be the main expressed or implied aims of development process to alter institutional arrangements for raising the income levels of the people in order to provide better living conditions to them. A paradigm on development with the focus on rural development has been formulated. It is based on five basic elements such as the institutional, technological, infrastructural, participative and human development service oriented changes to affect the social structure in terms of occupational diversification, social mobility, reduction in income disparities and changes in values and social relationships for an integrated social living and transformation of the society to a new social order (Mehta, 1984).

The transformation of the Mauritian nation-state which adopted democratic parliamentary system of governance after its independence, through different development initiatives and planned interventions, will be examined within the paradigm of the development, depicted above, focussing on institutional, technological, infrastructural, participative and social service oriented changes, while analysing and understanding the movement of this island nation from community to its societal formation.

Before we take up the changes observed in Mauritius on the above parameters towards a full-fledged societal formation, it may be apt to briefly touch upon the profile of this island nation. Its location in the Indian Ocean is strategically significant as it has raised the naval and maritime interests of big and powerful nations such as USA, France, United Kingdom etc. (U.S.A has a naval base in Diego Garcia, There is a dispute which Mauritius has with Britain over its sale and handing over to the United States of America). Moreover, it has bracing climate, beautiful beaches and undulated mountaneous ranges which makes it attractive to the tourists. Besides, sea food availability has drawn interest even from the Japanese and other investors in fishing business. Historically speaking, though it had no original inhabitants, but the early settlers were the European Whites (Dutch, French and British) who brought with them black slaves from Mozambique and Madagascar to cultivate land for the plantation of sugarcane in order to process it for the manufacture of sugar. The slaves, after the abolition of slavery on the island, were joined by Indians who were brought here by colonial regimes as indentured labourers (Both the Hindus and the Muslims). The former are known as African Creoles while the latter as Indo-Mauritians. Some Chinese, who took up trading subsequently and European whites, who were brought up by colonists (French and British) also formed part of the Mauritian population. Chinese are known as Sino-Mauritians while the whites are clubbed with the African Creole to constitute the population category of "General Population". The French whites are known as Franco-Mauritians. In fact, Mauritius represent a composite culture of Europe, Africa and Asia, as people drawn from these continents have their religious, linguistic, caste or sectional ties with that of their counterparts in their respective countries of immigration. Barring a few aberrations, Mauritius represents a nation, which despite of multiethnic, religious and linguistic composition has exhibited harmonious relationships between people of different origins.

The economy which was earlier based on stagnant agricultural production of sugar cane for processing and milling of sugar in the pre-independent and immediate post independent era, got a boost after the independence of the nation in 1968. Over a period of four decades, the Mauritius Country Report BTI 2008 (Bertelsmann Stifting Gutersloh: Bertelsmann Stifting, 2007) has shown that the country has acquired a status index of 8.33 in the scale of one (lowest) to 10 (highest) score. The market economy status index is 7.86 while the democracy status index is 8.80 in the same scale. Even, the demographic indicators including that of health status show remarkable achievements. The population size, which is 1.2 million, has been maintained at that level because of reduction in population growth, which has been kept at 1.1 percent per annum. The life expectancy of people has gone up to 73 years, which is fairly comparable with some of the developed nations. There is an increase in urban population, which is now 42.4 percent of the total population. The education Index is 0.81 while the Human Development Index is 0.80 (the highest being 1). On Human Development Index of 177 countries, it is ranked 63. Besides, the public expenditure on Education of GDP is 4.7 percent and on health it is 2.4 percent of GDP (UNDP, 2006, The World Bank, 2007).

The above indicators do speak positively about the well-developed social services like education and health. Even the social security measures are good to maintain the welfare of a large population, which is deprived, and remain at the sustenance level. The social and economic development of the nation, under the political economy based on democratic governance could accelerate the process of progress, advancement and growth, though the political system remained vulnerable to alliances and coalitions of different pre-and post independent political outfits. The political system evolved steered the process of transforming the country despite the factious nature of politics and struggle for power among leaders of different political parties who operated along religious, linguistics, caste and sect lines (The Management Index as per Mauritius Country Report is 7.23).

In the backdrop of the above scenario, let us highlight the changes observed in the institutional, technological, infrastructural, participative and social service oriented spheres of life. The institutional changes indicate transformation of economic, political and social life of people in Mauritius. We do observe that over a period of four decades, there has been tremendous transformation of economy in Mauritius as there has been diversification of it from the mono-crop of sugar cane for milling operations to manufacture sugar, to the manufacturing and garment industries promoted as a part of Export Processing Zones (EPZs) started by the nation-state for development of the country. These initiatives raised employment and income of the people on the island. This was further enhanced by tourist industry, fishing, tea and tobacco production. The real break-through in the Mauritian economy came as a result of "*Morcellement*" policy, which parcelled land to a large number of indentured labourers on the sugar estates to own land and acquire the status of small planters. Because of assured price of sugar in the world market under the *Lome* convention, the sugar estates (there were 21 sugar estates owned by whites (French and British). Only one was operating in the public-sector while 20 of them were managed in the Private sector) and nearly 30,000 odd small planters, witnessed sugar boom on the island. The profits accrued to sugar barons and small planters gave rise to construction boom and people, especially the small planters and other well off labourers and skilled workers, not only improved their housing conditions but also could afford to provide higher education to their children abroad. They, on return, were absorbed in the newly created positions in the Mauritian bureaucracy and expanding private and public sector undertakings.

Despite devaluation of Mauritian rupee twice during 1980s to comply with the Structural Adjustment Programmes of the World Bank and IMF to stabilize the economy, the nation-state through the expansion of EPZs, textile and garment industry, manufacturing industries, high end tourism, real estate business, beach resorts, hotels, restaurants, airways, express and highways etc. to meet the requirements of tourist industry and information technology, the establishment of cyber city and call centres, off shore banking, new financial and banking institutions, etc could steer the economic hurdles confronted and put the economy in good position. The GDP rose and the unemployment rate was on the decline, the export was up and the import cost was manageable and the balance of payment condition improved. In the 1990s, Mauritius was mentioned as a kind of economic "miracle" and was suggested as a role model to be followed by the African nations.

However, this economic transformation is not without pitfalls. The foremost pitfall is its shrinking agriculture based on the mono-crop of sugarcane. Due to declining interest in sugar produced from sugarcane and preference accorded to that produced by beet by the European Union (as sugar produced out of beet is cheaper than that produced from sugar cane) and other world economies, there is reduction in the number of sugar mills (Presently, these were only ten or so and within a couple of years, these shall be further reduced to six or so). The sugar estates in Mauritius are being asked by the European market agents to concentrate their activities on the limited number of mills to undertake milling operation of sugarcane for sugar production and supplement it with production of ethanol, molasses and other by-products of sugar. Besides, it is advised that a retrenchment policy of workers should be pursued by offering them Voluntary Retirement Scheme (VRS), which should include lump sum payment of amount proportionate to their period of employment and a small piece of land to construct a house as a part of the rehabilitation package. Even, the sugar barons, can enter into sale deeds with the state for certain development projects such as cyber city or tourist resorts, or for building express and high-ways etc.

This shift in agricultural economy towards a declining trend is also substantiated by a decline in the textile and garment industry as Mauritius is no longer, now being considered, as a preferred nation by the European and Western markets. This has resulted in an other kind of pitfall as many of the EPZs have been closed, resulting in raising the unemployment rate especially among the females who were mostly employed in these units (Nearly one third of the labour force employed in Mauritius are females and they are underpaid than their male counterparts). Many of these EPZs were jointly owned by foreign collaborators and Mauritian residents and after enjoying tax holiday benefits, some of them have left the enterprises. Besides, the import cost of materials needed to manufacture garments has gone up while the export demands have come down. These and a host of other factors, have made EPZs, a losing proposition.

Further, unlike sugar industry where a cess was imposed by the state on the sale of sugar proceeds to generate revenue, the tourist industry does not provide any mean of revenue earning but it does substantiate employment generation. This pitfall holds good even for information technology sector, which is being considered employment and income generating development initiative. Chinese have shown interest to establish themselves in the cyber city centres in order to act as launching pads for the African nations, though Indians are not too enthusiastic about it because of better market opportunities in other parts of the world. Both these high end economic initiatives (tourism as well as information technology) not only need a well developed infrastructure to support but also professionally qualified and competent manpower resource to strengthen and consolidate them. In order to make these ventures function effectively in Mauritian economy, the state has the onerous responsibility of preparing or hiring professionals who could manage these sectors profitably for the development of the society. Preparing professionals may not be an easy solution as many of the well qualified residents move out of the country to seek better employment opportunities abroad and those who stay back are not sufficient in number to match the requirements of the growing economy. The alternative of hiring expatriates from other nations in these fields may not be cost effective as the salary structure and incentive packages paid to them may be exorbitant and may act as a boomerang to the growing economy. This pitfall needs to be addressed judicially by the state planners and administrators.

With the prospects of sugarcane cultivation, processing zones of textile and garment industry on the decline and the future of tourist as well as information technology sector not very promising for the Mauritian economy, the way ahead perhaps is to get back to agriculture as the food crises is looming large on the island because of rising fuel prices (the cost of petrol in the world market, at the time of study had risen to $ 140 per barrel and that had affected the food stuffs imported from other countries. However, the cost, no doubt, has gone down to $ 70 or 80 also per barrel but the subsidized prices given to consumers, cannot offset the effect of its import substantially). The state must negotiate understandably with the sugar barons to identify cultivable land, being vacated by the sugarcane cultivations, to diversify agricultural operations, for the production of food articles like rice, pulses, milk by having good breed milching cattle, fish, mutton and chicken etc along with vegetables such as onions, potatoes, tomatoes, green leafy vegetables, capsicum, lady finger etc. to meet the consumption needs of the population on the island. The sugar barons must be convinced that instead of granting land parcels to workers under the voluntary retirement scheme and pay the lump sum amount, the land use may be changed to the advantage of food requirement for the people on the island. The state is seized of the problem and is exploring land for cultivation in the neighbouring states of Madagascar, Mozambique etc. but these joint ventures may not be cost effective in the long run. Instead the state should look inward for domestic production of food stuffs and through involvement of retrenched workers on the farms and the female workers in EPZs, and other manufacturing industries, the basic problem of food insufficiency can be salvaged adequately. Economists must realize that, no doubt, economics has a strong explanatory power for depicting production and consumption patterns of people, but it is weak in indicating distribution of resources and production assets. Some economists argue that the economic theory needs revision on that account. As such, the basic human needs like food, shelter, clothing, along with health care and educational services must be strengthened on a well-informed basis to tackle the problem of unemployment and poverty on the island.

The trickle down theory of economics as a capitalist ideology has been falsified for the developing nations. That is why, the political economists, have been raising hue and cry for effective ways of income distribution for the marginalized groups as a part of democratic governance which vouch for equality and social justice. In order to accomplish these goals, there is an urgent need to tackle another major pitfall which veers around a kind of collusion between political and bureaucratic elites on one side and that of economic elites such as sugar barons and wealthy merchants on the other. To make economic transformation a "miracle" for the Mauritian nation, there is a need to bring in greater transparency and accountability in development projects and their implementation. The Transparency International Corruption Index has ranked Mauritius at 42nd position, out of 163 countries in 2006. This shows that corruption is a serious problem and instead of establishing linkages between the polity and economy, as these sectors are held differently by separate ethnic compositions on the island, there is a need to encourage uncoupling between the two for fair distribution of resources to promote social justice and provide basic needs like food, housing, clothing etc to one and all on the island. Market economy has not shown its full manifestations and by denying its fruits of growth to all, it has remained imperfect.

The stability or instability of the political institution influences the development of a society. The political system evolved in Mauritius after its independence in 1968 has been that of democratic governance on the pattern of British Parliamentary System. Mauritius has seen tremendous struggle of its people against the colonist regimes to gain freedom while the multi-religious, ethnic and linguistic composition of its population contributed significantly towards it. The credit for gaining independence from British regime goes to Ramgoolam, a Hindu Physician, trained in medicine, in Britain. On his return to Mauritius after a decade, he joined the freedom struggle and with the support of other Hindu and Muslim political outfits (IFB and Comité dé Action Musalman), he as a leader of the Labour Party, succeeded in his ultimate efforts to bring freedom to the people on this island nation, despite stiff opposition from a conservative party led by a white in combination with the Creole population (Parti Mauricien Socialiste Democrate of Gautan Duval). This party opposed independence and was on the side of the British regime. Interestingly, the same political outfit supported the Labour Party led by Dr. Ramgoolam to form the government in the first post independent election held in 1976. This coalition government became a necessity in view of the emergence of the political party of the post independent era, that is, Mauricien Militant Mouvement (MMM) led by a French Marxist Paul Berenger who succeeded in wooing the youth and other radical unions or organizations to his side. MMM had almost swept the 1976 election and was to form the government but for the coalition support of PMSD to the Labour Party. This helped Dr. Ramgoolam to hold on to power and continue as Prime Minister. However, the coalition government was on a weak wicket. In the subsequent political elections on the island starting from 1981 to 2005, there emerged many political outfits which were based on ethnic, linguistic and religious lines to work out their political arithmetic to suit to their requirements of "win-win" situations.

Again, interestingly, the alliances between political parties were arrived at, before each election schedule, unlike in the pre-independent or in 1976 first post independent election. The coalition formed, (the term coalition and alliance are being used interchangeably here) whether on parity norm, mixed motives or on anti-competitive basis, by the political leaders of different parties, had a single goal of formation of government on the island and to hold on to power for effective decision making in the implementation of plans, schemes and projects for the growth and development of the Mauritian people. The significant observation in the political formation of alliances of different parties, is that the Fabian Socialism of Labour Party, the radical views of MMM and the conservative thinking of PMSD, as a part of ideological underpinnings were given a good-bye to the exclusive goal of winning the elections based on the well worked out political arithmetic of different political outfits. The democratic secular character of the parliamentary system of governance was weakened and the elections were fought on parochial or primordial ties of ethnicity, religious adherences and linguistic preferences of people. This has diluted the political institution of democracy and has reduced it as an imperfect one, which though encouraged liberalism but denied its participatory aspect to move towards the inclusive development of the Mauritian society. This segmental development has resulted in promoting social exclusion of certain-marginalized groups who need to be brought into the mainstream of the development milieu.

In fact, the desire to win election and hold on to power has been the single most motive of the power brokers. This has been evidenced clearly when a break group of strong MMM political radical outfit, formed another political party (Mouvement Socialiste Mauricien) led by a Hindu leader Anerood Jugnauth. This new formation showed its political acumen and dexterity by leading the people of the island through correct political arithmetic of different combinations and its leader Jugnauth continued to be the Prime Minister of the nation for thirteen long years. The only time a white Marxist Paul Berenger could share Prime Ministership with him, was his last position as Prime Minister for half the period. After that, he was elevated to the position of President of Mauritius, as it had attained Republic status by then and his son came forward to shoulder the responsibility of his party. The return of Labour Party to power in 2005 election with the support of ethnic, religious and linguistic groups led by Dr. Navin Ramgoolam (son of first Prime Minister Dr. Ramgoolam) who had lost power once, exhibits that politics is a game of strange bedfellows. This was also amply demonstrated in earlier elections when leaders of different political parties jumped from one bed to another to capture power.

Mauritius is encountering with an imperfect democracy, which is also demonstrated by the fact that there is social exclusion of women in politics. They are underrepresented in the political system across the board, Central, Municipal ,District and Village Council levels. Besides, the best loser system adopted in the Constitution of the country to accommodate minority communities is misconstrued and taken advantage of by the political outfits in power to stabilize their position in the system. Also, Media, which are considered the fourth pillar of democracy, are dominantly held by private players and political parties who vouch for their groups and project their images. This needs to be decentralized through the involvement cf grass roots organizations. Non-governmental organizations (NGOs) which are boon of a civil society are by and large, parasites on the nation-state as they mostly operate on the grants and subsidies obtained from the governments in power from time to time depending upon their political allegiances. Even local body administration (Municipal Council, District and Village Councils) is not fully decentralized as it is dependent upon the grants of the Central government. Without transfer of financial power to these bodies, decentralization will remain a far cry. In fact, decentralization within a centralized system of administration because of structural inconsistency of expected and performed functions, will make these local bodies dysfunctional. This adds to another dimension of imperfect democracy. The political system must respond adequately to the imperfections of democracy and bring in requisite electoral reforms and other institutional changes to provide good governance to its people.

It is a matter of fact that because of multi-ethnic, religious and linguistic composition of the population on the island, coalition politics will remain in vogue in future as well. The leadership will crystallize in persons having superior physical or mental traits, belonging to numerically dominant ethnic/religious/linguistic groups and having economic dominance in these groups. Besides, they should have the dexterity to take advantage of the situations in which they are placed (The present Prime Minister Dr. Navin Ramgoolam has shown maturity in providing a balancing act in the power game by appointing three Deputy Prime Ministers, each belonging to the three ethnic/religious/ linguistic groups (elite groups), one Muslim, the second Christian and the third a Tamilian).

The economic and the political differentiation processes pursued during the last four decades of independence in Mauritius should trigger off social transformation of the island nation. However, it is observed that the economic "miracle" or transformation has not affected the social organizational and structural arrangements among people adequately to register any significant change in the way of life of the people. There is reinforcement of ethnic identities of people belonging to their respective religious, linguistic and racial stocks. The Franco-Mauritian population is numerically not significant but economically it constitutes an elite class and maintains social distance from the Indo-Mauritians (Both the Hindus and the Muslims) who in comparison are less wealthier than the white population, but many of them have raised their social status to that of an emergent middle class, being qualified as professionals, bureaucrats and civil servants. However, there is a built-in mistrust, biases and prejudices developed between the Franco and Indo Mauritians. The Franco-Mauritians, have been observed to be tolerant towards the Sino-Mauritians and the white and African Creoles of the general population "Category" as they have a common thread of Christianity being pursued by them as a religion. As such, the Chinese and the African or White Creoles have better chances of being accommodated in the private sector than their counterparts belonging to the Indo-Mauritian ethnic groups.

The occupational diversification as a result of economic transformation has not brought about any substantial change in hierarchy of ethnic groups since class distinctions are still maintained along ethnic lines. The Franco-Mauritians, maintain the top position in the social stratification based on class dimension, followed by Chinese who being traders and merchants, are second in the ladder of class hierarchy, while the Indo-Mauritians (Both of the Hindu and the Muslim ethnic stocks) constitute the third layer of social class. The African Creoles are ranked last in the class hierarchy. There is resurgence and strengthening of ethnicity on the island because of the electoral system adopted as a part of parliamentary form of democratic governance based on adult franchise and the "Best Loser System" that takes care of the interest of the respective ethnic and minority populations.

Among the Hindus who are also divided linguistically along the horizontal plane, the caste divisions have been observed. There is hierarchy maintained between upper caste Hindus comprising of Brahmins and Kshatriyas (they constitute a smaller proportion) and the Vaishayas and the Raviveds who are on the lower end of the caste hierarchical ladder especially at the time of contracting of marriages between the persons of different caste groups. There have been inter-caste marriages observed especially among the Brahmins and Kshatriyas. However, Vaishyas constitute the bulk of the Hindu population, as such, not only this group has become significant in encouraging marriages within it but it has also acquired a distinction of throwing up Prime Ministerial candidate in elections because of its numerical dominance. The Raviveds who belong to the lowest castes, have, by and large, embraced Arya Samaj and are also a force to reckon with at the time of elections. Even, the Muslims are divided on sect basis and a allegiance to a particular sect is considered important in marriage circles. There are a few instances of marriage occurring between persons of the Hindu, Muslim, Christian or between Chinese and Muslims or Hindus or Whites etc but these are mostly attributed to the factor of personal choice based on love or more so as a class phenomenon depicted by the lifestyle of the partners.

In the above backdrop, one may venture to suggest that though changes in ethnic or racial relationships are not highly pronounced to acquire a secular character, yet, over the years, because of greater opportunities of mixing up of the different ethnic or racial groups due to economic transformation and occupational diversification on the island, there is better tolerance and acceptance of one group by the other. Even, the social stratification pattern is based on caste, sect or class dimensions and it is very difficult to suggest whether or not caste is being replaced by the class phenomenon. However, both the class and caste dimensions have been influencing the power structure, but the caste combination among the Hindus, who constitute nearly half the population, is observed to be significant in throwing up prime leadership in the country.

Howsoever strong may be the operation of primordial ties of ethnicity, religion, caste or sect, there is one departure observed in the language spoken at home. Over the years, there has been a marginal increase in the French and English being spoken at home, but there is an overwhelming increase in the use of Creole dialect (since it has not as yet developed a script to be considered as a language) at home. This development is taken both in the positive as well as in the negative sense. In certain quarters, it is believed that through the common usage of this dialect at home (Nearly 70 percent of people use it for conversation), a sense of solidarity among the Mauritians may be developed. This may be an asset in development of Mauritius as a society. On the other hand, as a vehicle of communication to transmit cultural traits and practices as values inherent in the respective ethnic groups to the younger generation of the people, this sets in distortion in the personality structure of young ones who are caught between the tradition and modernity. The ambivalent attitudes thus developed towards various aspects of social life may impel them to imbibe values close to Creole community. The Creolization process, thus set in, may dilute the ethnic identities of groups, which are struggling hard to keep them intact. For example, among the Hindus, especially those who embraced Arya Samaj cult, nearly half of them are finding it hard to refrain their children from taking non-vegetarian food and alcoholic beverages. Even the efforts made by the state and certain religious or linguistic organizations to promote Indian languages such as Hindi, Urdu, Tamil, Telugu, Marathi or Gujarati etc, their use at home during the last decade or so has been observed to be on the decline. This linguistic dilution is bound to affect the cultural core value system of the different ethnic groups, significant in institutionalising the social relationships built around institutions such as religion ,family, marriage etc.

Notwithstanding the above development which negates the maintenance of cultural values for their continuity to preserve and promote ethnic identities of various groups, it is observed that increasingly, the joint family structure is decomposing and giving way to the establishment of nuclear units. However, this nuclearlization process of families has not disbanded their relationships of nuclear members with that of core family members and they still maintain extension ties with them in time of crises and look towards them for help and need as and when it is required. Better occupational opportunities elsewhere on the island, economic independence of spouses (as most of the women are now employed as nearly one-third of the labour force is that of females), avoiding intra-familial disputes between mother-in-law and daughter-in-law, education of children and better life style, may be some of the reasons for choosing to have nuclear family establishments. Because of shortage of space, some of them among build up a living room accommodation on the first floor of the parent's house or in the adjoining vacant space. A multi-storey flat culture has been established in the cities on the island and lot of migrations from the rural areas, have taken place. Either, they have purchased or hired them to settle in there as nuclear units.

As mentioned earlier, marriage pattern, by and large, is based on the primordial ties of religion, language, caste or sect of different ethnic groups. Among the Hindus and the Muslims, the caste and the sect, have a lot of influence in marriage circles. Deviations, if any, on above lines in contracting marriages may be explained either as a class phenomenon or as based on "personal choice" of the partners. Serial marriages, live-in relationships, polygamous (polyandry as well as polygyny form) marriages and affording a "Mistress" or "Concubine", are, no doubt, on the increase but still they are not that significant to become a way of life on the island. However, because of better or improved status of women due to increasing education and employment opportunities as a consequence of economic transformation or development initiatives, the divorce rate is also on the rise. The main reasons for this being economic independence of women and assertiveness by them as a part of gender identity attained by them. This can be tackled only by having role complementarties of the spouses rather than enhancing role conflict between the genders. Sex education at the school, pre-marital and post-marital level marriage counselling and understanding each other's role is necessary, otherwise, the family as an institution will be shattered and the young ones will be devoid of protection, love and emotional support so necessary for a good society.

The institution of religion has a lot of influence on any ethnic group on the island. In fact, people, on their part, are less secular than their counterparts in other parts of the world. Though, the Constitution of the island-nation outlines the secular character of the state, yet in practice, the society at large is religious. Practically, all the fairs and festivals of different religious groups (Hindus, Muslims, Christians and Buddhists) are observed in a sacro-sanct manner and with great pomp and show. In that sense, Mauritius can suitably be called a nation of festivities, as the whole year around, one religious festival or the other is being celebrated. Interestingly, the festivals and the fairs, the rituals, customary practices and mythological depictions are not celebrated through the medium of the language of the respective religious groups exclusively but there is a mix of that with the Creole dialect. The dominance of "Creole" as a dialect is so pronounced that the public speeches made by political leaders on these functions, may begin, with Hindi or Urdu language but soon they switch over to "Creole". This is the dialect spoken and understood by the majority of population and has acquired the status of language **1** (one) on the island. Further, it was observed that even among the Tamils, Telugus, Marathis etc, not all understand their respective languages but while maintaining their linguistic identity, they communicate only in "Creole" dialect. This is a strange cultural contradiction observed. On the one hand, they want to continue with their religious festivals like Shivratri, Holi, Diwali, Cavadee, Id, etc. along traditional lines while on the other, they, especially the youth, pride themselves in the usage of "Creole" as dialect. They feel that by doing so, they are close to the Western developed French culture. This acquired cultural arrogance, perhaps, gives a greater sense of satisfaction to their respective egos by forgetting the racial discrimination confronted by them at the hands of the Whites.

However, while analysing the "Inclusion" of Indian Immigrants in Mauritius (as they constitute nearly 70 percent of the total population) within the Jaffery's (1980) "Multidimensional Model of Inclusion", focussing on core solidarity, ethnic out-groups and social differentiation process within a multi-ethnic society, Mehta (1989) points out that on the external axis of the model, Indo-Mauritians demonstrate a case of limited "inclusion" into the economic, social and religious sphere of the civil solidarity of Mauritius. It is only in the political sphere that they have made their mark in their struggle for political independence as well as in showing political domination in the post independence period. But, on the internal axis of the model, their race, kinship and religions have not allowed them from being included in the civil solidarity of Mauritius. The only factor that has contributed significantly to their "inclusion" into the civil solidarity is the spoken language, that is, "Creole", which is a commonly shared cultural trait of the masses in Mauritius. In short, the Indo-Mauritians present a case of uneven, "Inclusion" into the core solidarity and civil social set up of Mauritius.

No doubt, as stated by Childe (1957) in his classic work (What Happened in History) the real change is always uneven. It is a well-known fact that social change (not within revolutionary framework when it is observed to be sudden and abrupt), within an evolutionary perspective, is always slow and follows the path of least resistance. It will be fast in those social institutional arrangements where the inputs of change do not confront any counter change movements or barriers. However, like the flow of water, the change whether immanent or induced shall find directions, which provide least resistance to its flow of events or actions. To accelerate the process of social change or transformation of society, the forces of change, the direction of change and time span of change need to be intensified otherwise, there is always cultural lag observed between the fast moving high-tech economic system and the social structural and social organizational arrangements. Can the Mauritian political apparatus match the fast track of economic high-end technological and infrastructural growth and development with that of the Mauritian social institutional arrangements, to realize or accomplish Mauritius as a full-blown society?

Mauritius, as an island, is only connected through the sea and air routes, hence it is likely to be isolated and cut-off partially from the rest of the world. But its exploitation of the sea-economy in the form of "fish catch" as well as its beautiful and scenic beaches, has made it attractive for the tourists from across the world to visit it and enrich its way of life. Besides, bilateral and multilateral ties and relationships established by the vibrant Mauritian politico-economic system with other countries around the world and international funding agencies has made it a centre of social, cultural and economic activities. If we take into account the competitiveness and manufacturing exports indices worked out by the United Nations Report (2001), in 1998, Mauritius tops the list of African nations (Competitive Indicator of 97.1 and Manufacturing Exports of 1046.7) followed by Senegal, Algeria, Egypt and South Africa in that order. Thus the export oriented manufacturing economy of Mauritius has brought it into the centre-stage of the world dominant economies like that of countries of European Union, South Africa, France, U.K. and U.S.A. As such, its people have been exposed to the globalising experiences of other developed and even of the developing nations like China and India, and they have developed modern outlook and orientations. Besides, many banking and financial institutions and multinational corporations have made their presence felt by introducing new ways of life among the people. Their lifestyle has changed considerably and there is acculturating influences of "other" cultures in food habits, dress patterns, commercialisation and spread of western culture by electronic media, fast food chains like KFC, MacDonald, designers' wears, pubs, discos, casinos, growth of sex industry because of rise in tourism, decline in the use of ethnic languages, customs and practices and rise of use of French and English language, rise in manufacturing industries resulting in pollution, waste and other environmental and health hazards due to rise in fuel emissions of increased traffic volume of imported cars, trucks and buses. In fact, the globalising influences are largely negative and there is cultural invasion rather than cooperation of the western world.

We shall take up the infrastructural growth and the technological breakthroughs witnessed on the island. Over the last three or four decades, there is tremendous growth of infrastructure on the Island nation after its independence in 1968. There is complete modernization of sea-port and air-port and these have been raised to the international standards. Caudan waterfront with shopping arcade facing the seaport, looking scintillating in the night through its glittering lights, is stated to be built on the pattern of cape-town in South Africa. The Plaisance airport now rechristined as Sir Seewoosagur Ramgoolam, has been fully modernized with all the facilities to the travellers including a duty free shop. Port Louis, the capital of Mauritius, has virtually gone vertical, as the multi-storey buildings which house many banking, financial and bureaucratic institutions, besides offices of MNCs, private sector organizations and that of international organisations, dot the entire capital city. Traffic jams are frequent, especially during the peak hours of offices, as the volume and density of vehicles of all types has increased many folds.

Despite the four-lane highway leading to the capital city from other main cities and residential areas, the traffic congestion is huge and often results in traffic jams causing inconvenience to commuters who have to start early in the morning to reach offices and return late in the evening to get back to their homes. No doubt, public transport system has improved considerably by allowing the private bus service to operate with the National Transport Service, yet the fares charged to reach the destination of dis-embarkment are beyond the means of a common person. The enhancement in fare is attributed to free travel facility granted to senior citizens and the school going children since their travel cost is compensated by putting burden on the unemployed or employed adults. The pooling of cars is hardly done, as each one, because of easy loan facility, can own a deluxe car of one's own. There is a need to decongest the traffic jams and facilitate easy flow of traffic by constructing expressways, highways and flyovers over the congested points, identified on the island. The state apparatus should also seriously think about the spread of "on the surface" type of metro-rail line to provide better transport system to its citizens.

Apart from Port Louis becoming vertical in its architectural outlook, the other main cities like Rose-hill, Vacoas, Phoneix and Curepipe have also got a face-lift by having multi-storey buildings, apartments, shopping malls and arcades, cinema halls, theatres, pubs, restaurants and eateries etc. Traffic jams are observed on weekends and holidays as these places are frequently visited by people for shopping and buying daily needs. The body language of the people visiting these places appear to be casual, as most of them wear casual westernised dresses, look dandy and fashionable, have formal, self-oriented personalized behaviour pattern with rationalistic outlook of "hell with others" attitude. Among the Indo-Mauritians, the Hindus and the Muslims may have largely adopted western dress pattern, but some of them do like to look ethnic by wearing traditional dress code like "Kurta-Pyzama" or "Sherwani" etc. Among the Hindu women, the wearing of sari is on the decline and most of them wear them on special occasions while the daily wear dress is either marked by western type or "Salwar-Kameez" which was once a cultural symbol of Punjabi India. It is not only trans-Indian but has now become a trans-international dress as working women find it a more comfortable dress than a saree. However, many Muslims women still wear a long coat like dress with the head covered by a scarf to mark their ethnic identity.

Notwithstanding the above changes observed in the lifestyle of people as a consequence of infrastructural development, the other two important areas of infrastructure that affect people's life are power (energy) and water supply. Because of increased manufacturing, textile and garment industries, sugar milling operations, hotels, resorts and restaurants as a result of expansion of tourism, expansion of private and public institutions, schools, colleges, university, medical colleges, technological and engineering institutes, information technology centres (including call centres) and increasing use of electrical domestic cooking appliances and electronic goods etc., the power or energy requirement needs to be substantiated and expanded on the island. Power, so far, is being generated from coal thermal or fuel (oil) thermal plants. The rising cost of transportation of coal from South Africa and the oil imports, do not make power generation neither sufficient nor cost-effective. As such there is a need to identify the areas and exploit the renewable energy from the wind and hydro resources. Mauritius has potential for these resources and only a political will can make it possible to supplement these power resources, which are also eco-friendly and may contribute to sustainable development. For water supply, Mauritius depends upon rainfall. If it is insufficient, there is shortage of water supply as there are only two main reservoirs where rainwater, after required treatment, is supplied for home consumption. For irrigation of sugar cane plantations, sprinklers are employed which use raw water resource. There is a need to explore possibility of more water reservoirs and look up for sites where hydrological operations could be launched for pumping out water from the deep-water regions.

Technological breakthrough in Mauritius is hardly visible except perhaps in Sugar-Industry Research Institute. There is not much of R and D (Research and Development) to develop indigenous technology, responsible for the growth of Mauritian Society. By and large, it is transfer of technology that dominates, not only in the economic activities of manufacturing, sugar milling operations, cyber city centres including call centres, medical and engineering institutes, textile and garment industry, construction of hotel, tourist resorts, sea-port, airport etc, but also indirectly in the greater use of domestic appliances and electronic goods by the emerging middle class and upper class but it also affects the social and cultural life of people. In fact, there is modernization of technology and many technical innovations have been diffused among the people and they have in majority, adopted them. Those who remained laggards are now catching up the early adopters because of expansion of economy, rise in salary structure and employment of both the spouses. Women employment has necessitated the increased use of electrical domestic appliances like cooking range, rice cooker, washing machine, cooking gas etc. as these have proved time saving devices for them. Even in the construction of roads, buildings, highways, expressways, irrigation, mowing of lawns and maintenance of gardens, traffic lights, woodwork, furniture etc, modern equipments and gadgets are employed by the workers. There is greater reliance on capital (technical) intensive rather than labour intensive activities. This may be necessary because of shortage of skilled workers on the island. Many skilled workers have been hired from India, Bangladesh, Sri-Lanka, China etc. on contract, based on the issue of work-permits. However, the cost of technical equipments and gadgets may be prohibitive, because of their importation from the developed nations.

Participatory rather than liberal democracy should be the goal of good governance, as without the involvement of individuals and groups in the decision making bodies at the local level, democratic system does not strike its roots to tackle problems and issues confronted by one and all. As such, decentralization as a mechanism for inclusive development of different groups (religious, linguistic, caste, sect, ethnic based) becomes not only a sufficient but also a necessary condition. In Mauritius, besides a centrally elected Parliamentary System which has been well defined by a Constitution and evolved to tackle the macro-level economic and social problems of the people, there is a provision of local level administration through established Municipal Councils for Cities, District Councils and Village Councils, the elections to which are held on regular basis. However, these decentralized local bodies have to depend upon the central grant and subsidies as they hardly generate revenue of their own. Unless, there is a transfer of adequate funds to these local bodies from the central budget, they may find it hard to perform their functions to satisfy the needs and demands of the local people. In fact, decentralization process evolved for them through electoral system, functions within the centralized system of administration. As a consequence of this, they largely become dysfunctional. Even the mushrooming of Non-Governmental Organizations (which are considered a boon for the civil society) on the island, do not function adequately to tackle the local problems as most of them are fund starved and look towards central government for grants and subsidies. In fact, many of them have become a burden rather than asset to the state apparatus while others are used as instruments to mobilize people for political purposes before and at the time of elections.

Notwithstanding the above developments, participatory democracy to make development inclusive rather than socially excluded should be promoted, encouraged and practiced to distribute the fruits of development to one and all, irrespective of age, sex, income, caste, sect, religion or language. This may require suitable modifications in the Constitution as well as in the Electoral System of the nation-state.

On the social services front like education, health and social security measures such as old age and widow pensions etc., Mauritius as a nation-state stands tall among the other neighbouring nations in the African continent. However, despite expansion of education and health services on the island by the respective governments, both of these services are more a function of the income rather than that of human rights. Those who can afford can avail of these services in the private or private aided schools, colleges or private clinics or nursing homes, while a large majority of the population, depend upon the public aided government schools, colleges or over crowded hospitals. Further, rich or wealthy persons send their children for higher education in professional courses like medicine, law, engineering and accountancy abroad, while the others who cannot afford foreign education, have no option but to pursue higher studies in the local university (the only exceptions are the brilliant students who have been awarded scholarships to pursue higher studies in France, U.K., Australia etc.) In the early years of independence, there was a large outflow of students for higher education to India, which was relatively cheaper than France and U.K. But, now with the emergence of upper middle and middle class, even Indo-Mauritians want to send their children to Europe, Canada, U.S.A. and Australia etc. for higher education, as the education from these places is valued most and is considered prestigious to obtain good jobs in the back-home setting. Similarly, many of the economic and political elites prefer to have their medical problems treated in European and Britain hospitals.

No doubt, the social security measures have been well developed on the island, yet their management is not satisfactory. Many of the people who are needy and deserving get excluded because of bureaucratic red-tapism and favouritism. These measures, however, in a way, help in halting the process of sliding down of many people below the poverty line but the enlisting of beneficiaries under these measures and the distribution of resources need to be stream lined, made more transparent and accountable to promote equity and social justice, as a part of the welfare economics. Even, the education and health services on the island, need to be dispersed and distributed equally to the extent possible in providing social justice under democratic governance.

Movement from an Island Community to Society

On the basis of the structural differentiation processes observed, in economic, political and social institutional aspects delineated in the preceding pages, can we suggest that there is a shift indicated in the structure of Mauritius from an island community to that of society, with an increasing individuation of persons, a decline from a communitarian way of life of people or groups that has distinct institutions built around their core values systems and enhanced well defined institutional and regulatory systems that bring in more of rationalistic outlook, formal social relationships between different groups and individuals having self oriented goals, intentions, motives, aspirations and designs in a highly impersonalised structure which instead of moving into a civil society, may acquire the overtones of a "risk society" in the post-industrial scenario. Mauritius, no doubt, has not fully acquired as yet a post-industrial status but it has evolved elements that may lead it towards a risk society in the future.

A sociological analysis of human groups is generally confined to change and continuity of social structural or organizational arrangements based on the micro (an individual), meso (group or community) or on macro level (societal) examination. Of these three levels of analysis, the one based on micro (individual) or macro (societal) levels are given significant importance and the sociological theories are often developed around these dimensions while the meso level analysis, focussing on group or community dimension is marginalized.

Furnivall (1957) may argue that plural societies got formed as a result of colonial contact in the more recent times by freeing the local and international forces from social control and in turn, halting the development of social institutions, thereby creating a society without a social will. In such a society, separate racial groups exist, but each group is an aggregate of individuals rather than a corporate whole. Further, the social life of individuals is incomplete as members of the several groups intermingle and meet as individuals because these groups are not fully segregated to constitute a community having distinct institutions mediated by the core values inherent in them. However, this conception of plural society may not be relevant in the context of Mauritius. Perhaps, the conception of it, by Smith (1965), is more appropriate in delineating Mauritius as a composition of different groups or "communities" made up of distinct cultural institutions, distinguishing one from the other on the basis of core values upheld by them. The religious adherences of different communities to their respective faiths, and their interest and leanings to the languages of their origin, may make one believe, Mauritius as an Island community in the early years of its independence. But during the last four decades of its independence especially in 1980s and onwards, the economic transformation and political differentiation processes, have triggered off many changes that have not only affected the lifestyle of people but also the social institutional arrangements that are now patterned on the European or Western way of life.

No doubt, Mauritius, in the wake of globalisation is increasingly becoming a society with a complex of an overlapping process system wherein interaction of social persons and a number of interacting systems such as economic, religious, political, educational and other activities cohere together to form partially independent systems with units, boundaries and mechanisms of their own but overlapping with other societies on a broader range of spectrum of activities, yet there is a problem identified in the context of such a society with another grouping, that is, community. Community, as a concept, has been used in a variety of ways and needs to be distinguished from society. As stated earlier, some scholars consider communities as local based units of a larger society while others view them as depicting some aspect of society, especially related to its solidarity dimensions such as communal or spatial. But it is argued that the society is mainly maintained by its population through mating of persons of opposite sex, inhabiting a territorial area and indicative of permanent residence However, it needs to be recognized that the society is not the population alone but a complex system of action in which the units of population interact and participate. In the modern world, we have witnessed now the uprising of local traditional community based cleavages, which find a place for themselves through natural political systems or through the resurgence of respective diaspora of nation-states in the international arena across the national boundaries (Mayhew, 1968).

The community based cleavages or factions, which veer around ethnic solidarities based on religion, language, caste, sect etc. in the political system of Mauritius, cannot be ignored as they provide a strong linkage between individuals and society in the development milieu. As such, we shall examine not only the changes observed in Mauritius over the last four decades or so of independence at the individual or societal level but also at the level of solidarity groups or communities which mediate between the two and may facilitate or retard the process of formation of a good Mauritian society.

At the individual level, as has been evidenced by the analysis done in the preceding pages, people in Mauritius, by and large, have acquired self-oriented behaviour as a result of globalising and modernising influences. An individual shows personal orientations, is self-centred and his or her relations with others are formal has acquired mercenary rather than altruistic tendencies and is guided by his or her self interest rather than showing concern for others. In short, he or she has become a captive of his or her own thoughts, actions, intentions, motivations and desires based on his or her rational calculations to satisfy his or her own ego. This kind of individualization has subjected him or her to confront the increasing uncertainties thrown up by the world around. The individual in fact, is placed away from his or her social structure and becomes a victim of anxieties, guilt feeling, social sickness and of neurotic behaviour. Outwardly, he or she, may appear liberalized and independent but in reality, he or she is tied down by external forces and to mitigate this crises, he or she either seeks expert advice or takes inadequate decisions. Mauritians seem to be heading towards this kind of individualization, which Beck calls the symptoms of the "Risk Society" as a part of new modernity marked by economic prosperity, technological advancement and individual freedom along with hazardous environments. However, the individualization perspective leading to the emergence of a risk society beyond an industrial state is contested by Douglas who emphasizes that risks are culturally perceived as some people may identify certain hazards as risks while others may not do so. In short, notion of risk need to be expressed through cultural beliefs that people share and expect rather than based on individualistic judgements of the individual decision-maker.

But, Giddens views *risk society* more in terms of element of "security" syndrome since the science and technology has created new risks for human beings through simultaneously providing more opportunities for them to enjoy a secure and rewarding existence than were available in any pre-modern system. His argument is that 'late' modernity or high modernity entails uncertainties and an individual is likely to face a new risk at every step for which he or she finds it difficult to take a decision. However, he clarifies that the risk is not just a matter of an individual action but there are environments of risk that collectively affect large number of individuals. In traditional cultures, the risk environment was dominated by hazards of physical world and the nature while the modern risk environment is constructed by humanly created risks which he refers as "manufactured risks" mainly produced by the modernization process (Beck, 1992, Douglas, 1992, Giddens, 1991 as quoted by Sabbarwal, 2008).

In the above backdrop, if we analyse the growth and development of Mauritius towards the formation of society, we do observe that the modernization processes, engineered by improved infrastructural growth, macro-economic structures, banking and financial institutions, off shore trading and banking business, increasing international trade of exports and imports of goods, industrialization of sugar, textile and garment commodities, high end tourism and information technology sectors raising living standards of people matching to that of their European counterparts, and by having better educational and medical facilities, have moved the country beyond "take off" stage of development.

It is all set to become a postmodern society soon and may subject itself to a "risk society" marked by uncertainties and complexities.

Unlike in a societal formation where relationships are individualized, personal oriented, rationally determined, competitive in spirit and action, charged with the elements of dishonesty, sharp and corrupt practices and heightened by animosities, hatred and jealousies, the relationships in a community organization or social structure are invariably shaped or influenced by group norms and considerations, affective and cooperative orientations, bonds of affection, love, friendship and mutual aid or help, and dominated by principle of tolerance towards each other and concern for others etc. The values upheld by the various ethnic groups in Mauritius, may show a mix of both types in its transitional shift from Gemeinschaft to Gesellschaft way of life. However, a strong belief and attachment of people at large and especially those in rural areas of Mauritius to the cultural idioms, themes, values, norms and mores of their respective ethnic groups based on religious, linguistic, caste or sect dimensions, exhibit strong adherence to a communitarian way of life, reflective of their sense of identity formation. Barring language use, because Creole dialect has become dominant in the day to day life and has become a widely shared cultural trait, the Mauritians, are divided along religious lines while the Indo-Mauritians among them (Both the Hindus and Muslims) are stratified on caste and sect bases and adhere strictly to the values cherished within each caste or sect group especially in marriage circles and in establishing kinship ties. Even, the economic and political activities are influenced by such ethnic identities. This kind of social reality is visible in almost all the religious fairs, functions and festivals of different ethnic groups. Though, the state in its Constitution has proclaimed a secular character for its people, society, at large, is non-secular in its dispositions and actions. Further, there is not only gender discrimination observed in employment and wages but women are underrepresented in political life on the island. All such factors and many more inherent in the community social life characterized by traditions, may hamper the process of acquiring the societal status in respect of Mauritian nation-state.

Could we call Mauritius, on that account, a half-made-society, a concept that has been evolved by Meighoo (2008) for his study on *"Ethnic Mobilizaton vs Ethnic Politics in understanding Ethnicity in Trinidad and Tobago Politics"*. This concept may have limited application in the context of Mauritius as the social structure of the nation is not adequately affected by the economic transformation and political differentiation processes and is still determined by social institutional arrangements (Religion, ethnic identities, family and kinship networks, stratification based on gender, caste, sect or class dimensions and the traditional or quasi traditional marriage patterns). Even, this concept of "half-made society" may be difficult to operationalize for an empirical verification. As such, it may have limited utility.

Under democratic governance, the main goal of Mauritius as a nation-state is to move towards a civil society, characterized by a social organization that is rooted simultaneously in a radical individuation and a thorough collectivism. The social arrangements should move beyond the structure of economic equality often voiced in material sense but they should indicate social solidarity in universalistic terms, that is, in terms of "weness" of a national community which should transcend its particular commitments, loyalties and interests of various groups to forge a single thread of identity among the disparate people. If the above arrangement is established then one can conceive a community of society, the Gesellschaft as a

Gemeinschaft having collective consciousness and universal ties appealing to "impersonal" and highly generalized issues such as rights and peoplehood (Jaffery, 1990).

Further, it is mentioned by Jaffery (1990) that the mechanisms by which the civil society regulates the struggle for power and interest is law ramified through the enactment of Constitution which should take into account legal codes, institution of "office", symbolic code or language articulating universalistic ties, cultural codes to represent peoples' expectations, denial to a particular person or group an absolute power and reinforcement of universalistic regulations that a office and the Constitution provides. These mechanisms can provide a framework to the power elites to function in a pluralized manner and move the people towards a civil society.

But Jaffery, considers them as ideals and cautions that it may not be possible to create universal brotherhood of society itself. We may move only towards a restricted sphere of civil society. He opines that neither capitalism nor socialism can eliminate the competition for scarce resources and every struggle to acquire them may result in giving rise to instrumental and anti-normative dimensions. Even the struggle by elites for power and interest may not get eliminated as that may be determined by the convergence or dis-convergence of their interests with people at large. These pitfalls to civil society shall have to be examined in respect of every nation-state. In fact, he points out, that more a civil society gets institutionalised, the more do scandals, affairs and crises become a fact of social life. The main issue is not whether such tensions are created or not but how they are resolved to maintain the integrity and continuity of the civil society (Jaffery, 1990)

In the wake of the above dangers of a civil society identified by Jaffery, Mauritius as a nation-state, has to seize itself with the social, economic and political transformation of the country which is tiny in size but is embedded with complexities and uncertainties thrown up by historical circumstances, entangled social and economic inequalities because of skewed distribution of land resources, lack of highly qualified technologists, professionals and skilled manpower resources to manage high-end enterprises in Information Technology, tourism and modernization of industry, limited power generation, food shortages, scarcity of water supply for domestic consumption purposes, and factious nature of politics that brings in more dissensions than consensus between powér elites etc. These complexities and uncertainties need to be tackled by the power elites on a well-informed basis to make Mauritian Society (Gesellschaft) as Community (Gemeinschaft) or to have a community of society by building up a solidarity nation representing the people of individuals having collective consciousness and "impersonal" appeals. To move towards civil society, the nation-state must promote communitarian values such as tolerance, conciliation, sympathy, affection and warmth expressed through sentiments, belief in almighty God, mutual help, cooperation, and concern for needy and suffering and curb down the globalising and modernising values such as cut throat competition, individualism, jealousy, hatred, conflict, rudeness, self orientation and materialism. Besides, the national leadership should encourage wider participation of people in public affairs, eliminate ethnic discrimination, avoid the tiered economy of the rich and poor, preserve local culture and enlarge mass media openings to encourage local participation, expand health and education services-especially for the weaker sections of the society (Mehta, 1997). For all this to happen, th political will of the leadership structure is a necessary pre-requisite and the Mauritian national leadership, being vibrant and enlightened, may seize every possible opportunity to implement the above measures for the establishment of a civil society, which like Marxian socialism is a utopian concept but it needs to be pursued as an end goal for the realization of a good society.

References

Bertelsmann Stifting BTI 2008 (2007) *Mauritius Country Report*, Gutersloh, Bertelsmann Stifting.

Beck, Ulrich (1992), *Risk Society, Towards a New Modernity*, New Delhi, Sage Publications.

Childe Gordon, (1957), *What Happened in History*, Harmonds North, Middlesex, U.S.A. Penguin Books Ltd. (Reprinted) p. 282.

Dag Hammarskjold Report in Development and International Cooperation (1975), "To set in Motion the Process of Change", *Development Dialogue*, p. 7.

Douglas, Mary (1992), *Risk and Blame: Essays in Cultural Theory*, London, New York: Routledge.

Furnivall, J.S. (1939), *Netherlands India: A Study of Plural Economy*, Cambridge, Cambridge University Press.

Giddens Anthony, (1991), *Sociology*, Cambridge, Polity Press.

Jaffery, Alexander (1980), "Core Solidarity, Ethnic Out group and Social Differentiation: A Multidimensional Model of Inclusion in Modern Societies" in J. Dofny and A. Kiwowo (Eds). *National and Ethnic Movements*, London, Sage Publications.

Jaffery, Alexander (1990), "Democracy and Civil Society" (Draft Chapter) in his *Watergate and the Discourse of Civil Society*, Los Angeles, Department of Sociology, University of California.

Johnstone Ronald L (1988), *Religion in Society*, (Third Edition) New Jersey, Prentice Hall Englewood cliffs.

Mayhew, H. Leon (1968), "Society" in *International Encyclopaedia of Social Sciences* (Ed.) Sills, David L, Vol. 13, N.Y. the Macmillan Company and the Free Press pp 577-585.

Meighoo, Kirk (2008), "Ethnic Mobilization vs Ethnic Politics: Understanding Ethnicity in Trinidad and Tobago Politics" *Commonwealth and Comparative Politics* 46:1, pp. 101-127.

Mehta, S.R. (1984) *Rural Development Policies and Programmes: A Sociological Perspective*, New Delhi, Sage Publications.

Mehta, S.R. (1989) "The Uneven Inclusion of Indian Immigrants in Mauritius", *Sociological Bulletin*, Vol 38. No. 1, March Reproduced in Jayaram, N (2004) (Ed). *The Indian Diaspora: Dynamics of Migration*, New Delhi, Sage Publications.

Mehta, S.R. (1987) "Backwardness and Civil Society" in Mehta S.R. (Ed.) *Poverty, Population and Sustainable Development: Essays in Honour of Professor Victor S. D'Souza*, Jaipur and New Delhi, Rawat Publications.

Sabbarwal, S (2008). *Risk Society, Reflections on its Conceptualisations*, Chandigarh, Department of Sociology, Panjab University, (Mimeograph).

Smith, M.G. (1965), *The Plural Society in the British West Indies*, California, University of California Press.

The World Bank (2007), *World Bank Indicators*, Washington D.C.

United Nations Development Programme (2006), *Human Development Report*, New York.

United Nations (2001), *Economic Development of Africa: Performance, Prospects and Policy Issues*, New York, United Nations Conference on Trade and Development.

Index

C

T